The Art of Boutis

20 French Quilting Projects

Kumiko Nakayama-Geraerts

Photography: Fabrice Besse
Design: Sylvie Beauregard

STACKPOLE
BOOKS

0 11557 01288 0

Boutis: A pure white sculpture

For me, Provençal quilting, also known as boutis, is the emotion instilled by the beauty of French culture—its shapes, colors, scents, customs, and traditions. Since the 17th century, this craft has been admired and practiced in the south of France. Unfortunately, since the beginning of the last century, with the appearance of sewing machines and the changes in our lifestyle, this art has gradually been forgotten. Yet there is nothing more joyous or more beautiful to make as a gift for a marriage or birth.

With Provençal boutis, it is not only the beauty of working with textile that moves me but the cultural heritage associated with it, which has simultaneously opened doors to the past and to the present for me. I discovered this embroidery technique when I was working as a stylist for a fashion house. At that time, I didn't know that one day I would do it by hand myself. But it captured my spirit. It was through interior decoration that I first ran my fingers across a boutis pattern. It was an old piece which had taken on the colors of time—a little faded, a little muted. It held different messages: the soul of the people, the object's reason for being, the meaning of the motif.

This is a type of needlework that does not disappear but perpetuates life. An art that conveys both the beauty and richness of folk art. An art that allows you to transform a simple piece of cotton into a jewel.

And yet, nothing is clearer than these two fine fabrics stitched together by hand and embroidered with a raised motif. For anyone who wants to start or master this art form, in this book I suggest easy-to-make projects for items that you can use in your daily life or give as original gifts.

Kumiko Nakayama-Geraerts

Contents

Boutis patterns not included in these pages, along with sewing patterns, can be found on the detachable pattern insert at the back of the book.

Boutis
for Special Occasions

Supplies

- 2—15¾ x 20 inches white cotton batiste
- 2—15¾ inches white satin ribbon, ⅓ inch wide
- 1 spool white quilting thread
- 1 skein white embroidery floss
- ⅓ ounce cotton stuffing

Size: 3 to 6 months
Patterns on opposite page

Transferring

On one of the pieces of batiste, transfer the three patterns twice, spacing them 1½ inches apart (trace the pattern through the fabric, as explained on page 118).

Stitching

Place the blank piece of batiste under the prepared piece, wrong sides together. Baste them together (see page 118), then place them in an embroidery hoop (see page 120).

Embroider the flowers and hearts in backstitch with embroidery floss, the lines in running stitch with quilting thread, and the edgings in buttonhole stitch with embroidery floss (see pages 124–125).

Cut out the eyelets at the ends of the button loops to thread the ribbons through, then go around them in buttonhole stitch with embroidery floss.

Stuffing

Turn the work over to the wrong side. Stuff the flowers, hearts, and strips marked out by the lines (see pages 122–123).

Cutting

Cut out the six pieces close to the buttonhole stitches, leaving a ⅜ inch seam allowance along the outer perimeter of the uppers (including heels).

Assembling

In the front of the uppers, make a dart by folding the two purple dotted lines in the pattern against one another. Sew it in place with a small stitch on the wrong side (diagram 1). At the back, assemble the ends with ladder stitch and make a rolled hem (see page 126).

Sew small running stitches through the seam allowance along the outer edge; pull the thread to gather the piece, then fasten off (diagram 2).

Pin the uppers around the soles, right sides together. Assemble them with ladder stitch, sewing along the first line of boutis on the upper and just above the buttonhole stitches on the sole. Make a rolled hem on the seam allowance.

Turn the booties over on the right side. Pin the button loops at the back of the uppers, making them slightly overlap the uppers and matching up the pattern's purple * and ** marks. Assemble them with ladder stitch.

Finishing touches

Wash the booties. While they are still wet, fill them with scraps of cloth or crumpled handkerchiefs to give them a well-rounded shape. Let them dry in this shape.

Thread the ribbons through the eyelets of the button loops, evening them out on either side, then tie a bow in the front.

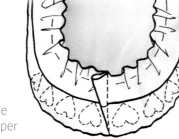

1. Making the dart at the tip of the upper

2. Gathering of the bottom of the upper

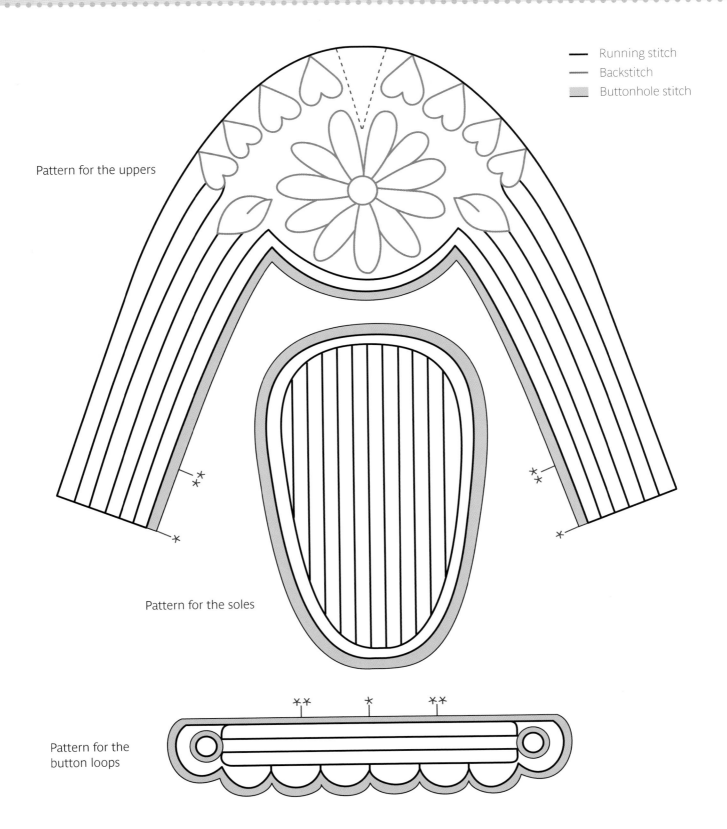

Running stitch
Backstitch
Buttonhole stitch

Pattern for the uppers

Pattern for the soles

Pattern for the
button loops

Running stitch
Buttonhole stitch

½ pattern for the bib
Make a mirror image on both sides
of the dotted line.

Supplies

- 2—12 x 15¾ inches white cotton batiste
- 35½ inches white cotton bias tape, ¾ inch wide
- 2—15¾ inches white satin ribbon, ⅜ inch wide
- 1 pearly white button, around ⅜ inch diameter
- 1 spool white quilting thread
- 1 skein white embroidery floss
- 1 ounce cotton stuffing

Size: 3 to 6 months
Pattern on opposite page

Transferring

Transfer the pattern to the center of one of the pieces of cotton batiste, making a mirror image on both sides of the dotted line, tracing the pattern through the fabric (see page 118).

Stitching

Place the blank piece of batiste under the prepared piece, wrong sides together. Baste them together (see page 118), then place them in an embroidery hoop (see page 120).

Embroider the motifs and lines in running stitch with quilting thread, then the scalloped edging in buttonhole stitch with embroidery floss (see pages 124–125).

Stuffing

Turn the work over to the wrong side. Stuff all the areas outlined by the stitching (see pages 122–123).

Cutting

Cut out the piece close to the buttonhole stitches of the scallops, leaving a seam allowance of ¼ inch on the rest of the edge.

Assembling

Pin the bias tape around the sides and neck of the bib, right sides together, close to the boutis. Sew along the edge. Clip the seam allowances ⅜ inch, close to the stitching. Fold the bias on the wrong side, then refold it with wrong sides together. Pin it, then sew it with slip stitches.

Finishing touches

Wash the bib, then let it dry.

Sew the button on at one end of the neck. On the other end, make a button loop with the embroidery floss, as explained on page 126.

On the wrong side, pin, then sew the ribbons on each side of the bib, above the last scallop (diagram below).

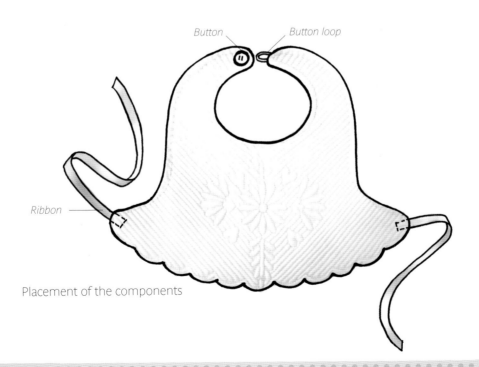

Button   Button loop

Ribbon

Placement of the components

Supplies

- 2—13¾ x 15¾ inches white cotton batiste
- 27½ inches white satin ribbon, ⅜ inch wide
- 1 spool white quilting thread
- 1 skein white embroidery floss
- 1 ounce cotton stuffing

Size: 0 to 3 months
Pattern on opposite page

Transferring

Transfer the pattern to the center of one of the pieces of cotton batiste, making a mirror image on both sides of the dotted line, tracing the pattern through the fabric (see page 118).

Stitching

Place the blank piece of batiste under the prepared piece, wrong sides, together. Baste them together (see page 118), then place them in an embroidery hoop (see page 120).

Embroider the motifs and lines in running stitch with quilting thread, then the scalloped edging in buttonhole stitch with embroidery floss (see pages 124–125).

Stuffing

Turn the work over to the wrong side. Stuff the motifs and strips marked out by the lines (see pages 122–123).

Cutting

Cut the piece close to the buttonhole stitches of the scallops, leaving a seam allowance of ⅜ inch on the rest of the perimeter.

Assembling

Bring the side panels B and C edge to edge with the center part A (diagram below). Pin them, then sew the edges together with ladder stitch (see page 126).

On the wrong side, make a rolled hem on each of the seam allowances (see page 126).

On the right side, sew the center of the ribbon folded in half to the bottom of the bonnet, at one of the ends. Make a button loop opposite the ribbon (see page 126).

Finishing touches

Wash the bonnet. While it is still wet, fill it with scraps of cloth or crumpled handkerchiefs to give it a well-rounded shape. Let it dry in this shape.

Thread one of the ends of the ribbon through the button loop, then tie it to the other.

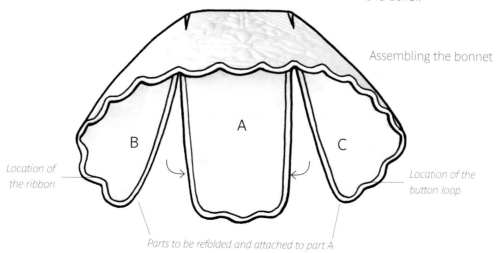

Assembling the bonnet

A

B

C

Location of the ribbon

Location of the button loop

Parts to be refolded and attached to part A

½ pattern for the bonnet
Make a mirror image on both sides of the dotted line.

— Running stitch

▨ Buttonhole stitch

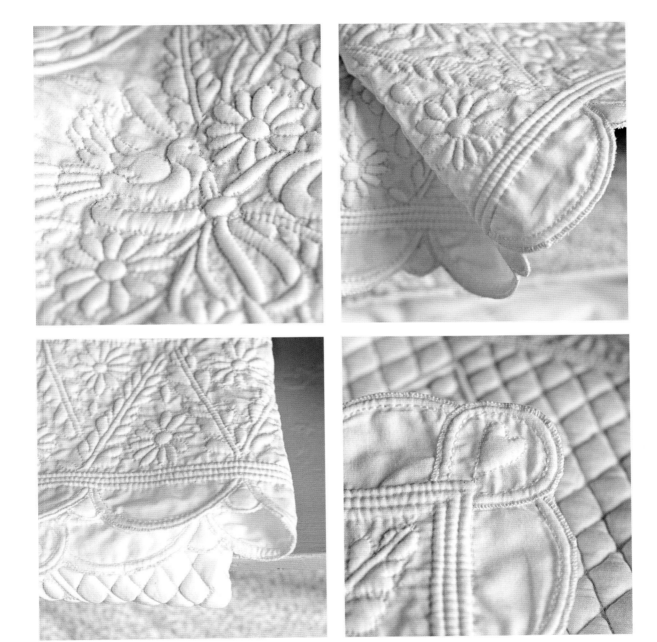

Supplies

- 2—35½ x 35½ inches white cotton batiste
- 1 spool white quilting thread
- 3 skeins white embroidery floss
- 5¼ ounces cotton stuffing

Dimensions: 27½ x 27½ inches
Patterns on opposite page and on the detachable pattern insert at the back of the book

Transferring

On one of the squares of batiste, using a ruler, draw the horizontal and vertical axes to determine where the center is. Tracing the pattern through the fabric (see page 118), transfer the diamond to the center, then repeat the border and edging on the four sides. Draw a lattice of lines slanted at 45° and spaced ½ inch apart in the empty space, criss-crossing them perpendicular to the diamond's angles (diagram below).

Stitching

Place the blank piece of batiste under the prepared piece, wrong sides toge-ther. Baste them together (see page 118), then place them in an embroidery hoop (see page 120).

Using quilting thread, embroider the motifs and lines from the inside with running stitch, then the lines and the hearts in the edging with backstitch; with embroidery floss, make the scallops on the border with buttonhole stitch and the dove's eyes with flat satin stitch (see pages 124–125). To embroider the medallions evenly on the border of the diamond, see the tip on page 59.

Stuffing

Turn the work over to the wrong side. Stuff the motifs, strips, and details of the frames, as well as the diamonds of the center panel, including the medallions (see pages 122–123).

Finishing touches

Wash the quilt. Cut the cloth close to the buttonhole stitches.

Placement of motifs

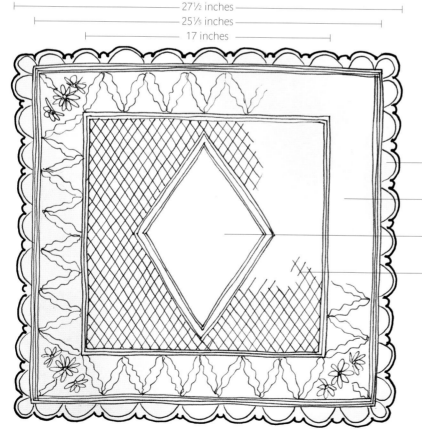

27½ inches
25⅛ inches
17 inches

— Edging (pattern on opposite page)

— Border (pattern in the detachable pattern insert)

— Diamond (pattern in the detachable pattern insert)

— Lattice of diagonal lines spaced ⅗ inch apart

Tip

For a project of this size, it is best to use a quilter's hoop for the stuffing. It is bigger and thicker than an embroidery hoop and will make your work easier.

Pattern for the corners of the edging

Repeat in the four corners of the rectangle, then fill the spaces around the edge by repeating the scallops (nine on each side).

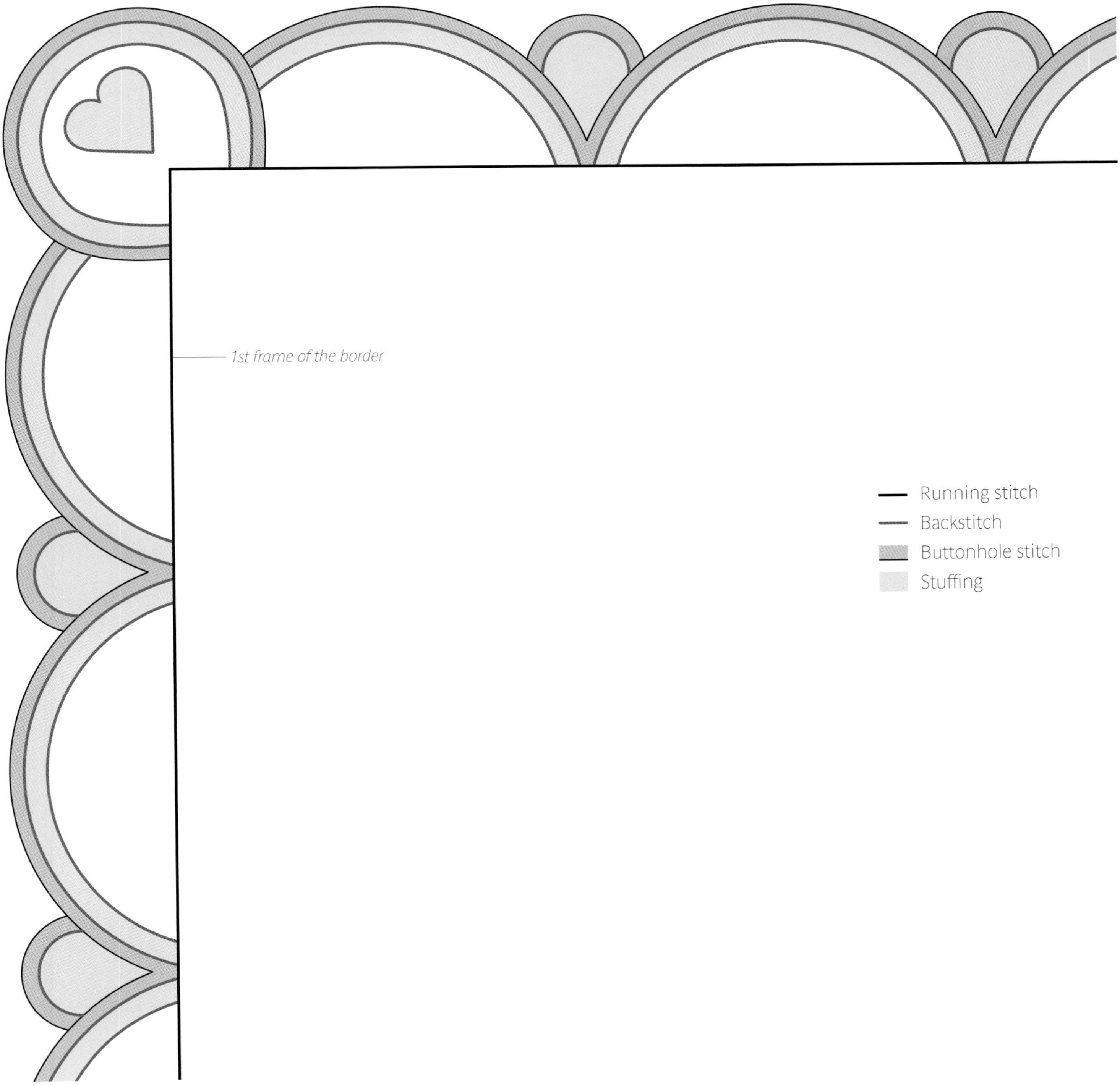
1st frame of the border
Running stitch
Backstitch
Buttonhole stitch
Stuffing

Supplies

- 2—13¾ x 13¾ inches solid purple cotton fabric (collar)
- 43½ x 59 inches purple cotton print fabric (main pieces, facings, and bias)
- 13¾ x 13¾ inches thin iron-on interfacing
- 2 snap fasteners, ½ inch in diameter, that can be covered in fabric (the part of the snap with the hole should be curved)
- 2 pearly buttons, ⅜ inch in diameter
- 1 spool purple quilting thread
- 1 skein purple embroidery floss
- ⅓ ounce cotton stuffing
- Purple sewing thread

Size: 12 to 18 months
Pattern for the collar, page 25; patterns for the main pieces and facings on the detachable pattern insert at the back of the book

Collar

Transferring

Transfer the pattern for the collar to the center of one of the squares of solid fabric, making a mirror image on both sides of the dotted line; trace the pattern through the fabric or, if the fabric is too opaque, use transfer paper (see page 118).

Stitching

Place the blank solid fabric under the prepared piece, wrong sides together. Baste them together (see page 118), then place them in an embroidery hoop (see page 120).

Embroider the petals of the small flowers and the leaves in running stitch with quilting thread (see pages 124–125). Then use embroidery floss for the large flower in the center and the rosette (backstitch), the centers and stems of the small flowers (stem stitch), the dots (satin stitch), and the scallops on the edging (buttonhole stitch).

For the center of the large flower, make a *rosette de Camargue* with the embroidery floss (see below).

Stuffing

Turn the work over to the wrong side. Stuff all the motifs outlined in running stitch and backstitch (see pages 122–123).

Finishing touches

Wash the collar. Cut the fabric close to the buttonhole stitches, leaving a seam allowance of ⅜ inch all along the inside edge.

Rosette de Camargue

Embroider the circle in blanket stitch, then cut out the inside. Embroider eight loops of equal size around the circle, interlacing each with the preceding one, then interlacing the last with the first (diagram 1). Wind the thread several times around each loop to make it more rigid (diagram 2), then strengthen the circle in the middle in the same way. Note that the diagrams opposite only have six rings for the sake of clarity, but the principle is the same.

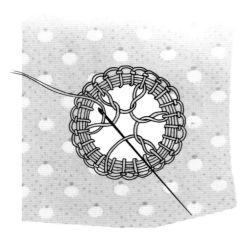

Diagram 1

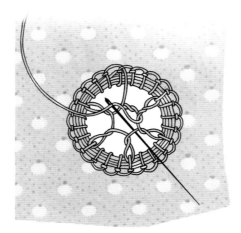

Diagram 2

Drxss

Preparation

Fold the print fabric in half, right sides together. Transfer the patterns for the front and back, aligning them on the fold. Cut these pieces out, leaving an allowance of 1¼ inches at the bottom and ⅜ inch on the rest of the perimeter. Oversew the edges with zigzag stitches.

Transfer the two lining patterns to the interfacing, inverting them to make a mirror image on both sides of the dotted lines. Cut these pieces out. Using an iron, fuse the pieces to the back of the remaining print fabric. Cut the fabric, leaving a seam allowance of ⅜ inch all the way around.

Assembling

On the right side of the front, make two pleats, folding the B marks to the A marks of the pattern. Pin them, baste them, then sew them close to the fold. Pleat the back in the same way.

Place the front on top of the back, right sides together. Pin the sides and the shoulders. Baste, then sew ⅜ inch from the edges. Open the seam allowances with the iron.

Pin the back facing to the ends of the front facing, right sides together, matching up the pattern's * marks. Baste, then sew between the marks ⅜ inch from the edges (that is, close to the interfacing). Open the seam allowances with the iron. On the outer perimeter, fold the fabric back to the wrong side ¼ inch twice, in order to

fold it over the interfacing. Iron, baste, then hem.

With the print fabric, make a strip of bias tape measuring ¾ x 3¼ inches (see page 126). Fold it in half, wrong sides together, and sew along the long side close to the edge. Fold it in half and baste its ends edge to edge to make a button loop.

Pin the lining pieces around the neck and along the slit in the back with right sides together. Insert the button loop at the top the slit. Baste, then sew ⅜ inch from the edges. Clip the seam allowances at regular intervals around the curves. Fold the linings over to the wrong side and sew them down by sewing through both layers all around the edge of the opening (diagram below).

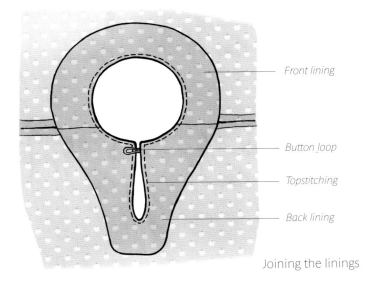

Front lining

Button loop

Topstitching

Back lining

Joining the linings

Armholes

With the print fabric, make two lengths of bias tape measuring ¾ x 15¾ inches. Pin them around the armholes, right sides together. Fold the excess on the ends to the wrong side, and trim it ⅜ inch from the fold. Baste, then sew ¼ inch from the edge. Clip the seam allowances at regular intervals. Fold the biases in half with wrong sides in. Fold back ¼ inch, wrong sides together, and baste them. Make a double topstitch around each armhole.

Hem

Fold back the lower edge of the dress ¼ inch to the inside, then 1 inch. Iron, baste, then sew ¹⁄₁₀ inch from the first fold.

Finishing touches

Sew a button at the top of the slit on the back of the dress, opposite the button loop, and another at the back of the collar. Make a ⅜ inch button-hole opposite it (see page 126).

Cover the snap fasteners with print fabric (see below). Sew a covered half to the center of each shoulder seam. Sew the second part opposite on the underside of the collar, making sure to go through only one layer of fabric. Attach the collar to the dress with the snaps. It is detachable, which is a practical feature.

Covering a snap fastener with fabric

On the part of the snap with the hole, place a round piece of fabric, slightly larger than the snap so that it covers the hole. Fold the loose fabric over the back and press to attach.

½ pattern for the collar
Make a mirror image on both
sides of the dotted line.

—— Running stitch
—— Backstitch
▬▬ Stem stitch
◍ Satin stitch
▬ Buttonhole stitch

Rosette de Camargue

Baby Gifts

Supplies

- 10¼ x 6¾ inches solid purple cotton fabric (outside)
- 10¼ x 6¾ inches white cotton batiste (lining of the boutis)
- Purple cotton print fabric (inside): 4—5 x 6½ inches (frames); 2 x 6 inches (edge)
- Medium-thick batting: 2—4 x 5¾ inches; ⅜ x 6 inches
- 1 skein purple embroidery floss
- ⅓ ounce of cotton stuffing
- Cardboard, about ¹⁄₁₀ inch thick (see cutting instructions opposite)
- Cardboard, about half as thick as the first piece (see cutting instructions opposite)
- 2—4 x 5¾ inches transparent plastic film
- Double-sided tape
- Vinyl fabric adhesive
- All-purpose adhesive

Dimensions of the closed frame:
  4¼ x 6 inches
Patterns on page 30

Cutting instructions

Cardboard, about ¹⁄₁₀ inch thick
- 2—4⅜ x 6 inches (A pieces)
- 1—⅜ x 6 inches (piece B)
- 2—4 x 5¾ inches (C pieces);
- cut a window out of the center
- (3 x 4½ inches).

Cardboard, about half as thick as the first pieces
- 2—4 x 5¾ inches (D pieces)

Transferring

On the solid fabric, baste a vertical line to mark the middle of the long sides. Transfer the flower motif to the center of the left half and the bear motif to the center of the right half. Trace the pattern through the fabric or, if the fabric is too opaque, with transfer paper (see page 118). Add the first name and the date using the alphabet on page 31.

Stitching

Place the batiste under the prepared solid fabric, wrong sides together. Baste them together (see page 118), then place them in an embroidery hoop (see page 120).

  With the embroidery floss, embroider the motifs in backstitch, the bear's eyes and nose in satin stitch, and the inscriptions in stem stitch (see page 124).

Stuffing

Turn the work over to the wrong side. Stuff the motifs (see pages 122–123).

Washing

Wash the piece, let it dry, then iron the unembroidered areas.

Putting on the cover, preparing the frames, and assembling

Follow the explanations for Wedding Memories, pages 38 and 39. When you put the cover on, cut the strip intended for the edge so that it measures 5¾ inches.

Supplies

- 17¾ x 15¾ inches solid sky blue cotton fabric (outside)
- 2—6 x 6 inches white cotton batiste (lining of the boutis)
- Striped sky blue cotton fabric: 14¼ x 10¼ inches (inside); 2—7 x 10¼ inches (flaps)
- 17¾ x 15¾ inches medium-thick batting
- 1 spool sky blue quilting thread
- 1 skein sky blue embroidery floss
- ⅓ ounce cotton stuffing

Dimensions of the closed health record cover: 6½ x 9½ inches
Patterns on page 30

Transferring

On the solid fabric, baste a vertical line to mark the middle of the long sides. Transfer the flower motif to the center of the left half and the bear motif to the center of the right half. Trace the pattern through the fabric or, if the fabric is too opaque, with transfer paper (see page 118). Add the first name and the date (alphabet on page 31).

Stitching

Pin the two squares of batiste under the prepared solid fabric, wrong sides together, centering them under the motifs. Baste them together (see page 118), then place the piece in an embroidery hoop (see page 120).

With the embroidery floss, embroider the motifs in backstitch, the bear's eyes and nose in satin stitch, and the inscriptions in stem stitch (see page 124).

Stuffing

Turn the work over to the wrong side. Stuff the motifs (see pages 122 – 123).

Quilting

Centering the two motifs, draw a frame measuring 13½ x 9½ inches on the piece, a second ¼ inch toward the inside, and four vertical lines spaced 1 mm apart to mark the edge. Also draw quilting points: space them ½ inch apart and stagger them from one line to the other (diagram below).

Pin the batting under the piece, then baste them together. With the quilting thread, embroider the quilting points through all layers, making four small, overlapping running stitches for each. Then embroider the frame and the edge with running stitch.

Cutting

Wash the piece. Cut the fabric, leaving a seam allowance of ¾ inch all the way around the frame.

Assembling

Fold each flap in half, wrong sides together, to get a 3½ x 10¼-inch rectangle. Baste the three open sides. Center the large rectangle of striped fabric on the quilted piece, with the wrong side against the batting. Align the long basted sides of the flaps. Pin the perimeter, baste it, then sew it with running stitch, close to the edge, making sure you sew through the batting and don't drift to the outside of the piece.

Fold the edge of the solid fabric over the striped fabric and sew them together by making a rolled hem (see page 126).

Quilting

⅗ inch

6½ inches — 6½ inches

9½ inches

13½ inches

Picture Frame
Child Health Record Cover
Motif for the right half

— Backstitch
▬ Stem stitch

Picture Frame
Motif for the left half

Child Health Record Cover
Motif for the left half

a b c d e f g h i j k l
m n o p q r s t u v
w x y z

A B C D E F G H
I J K L M N O
P Q R S T U V W
X Y Z

1 2 3 4 5 6 7 8 9 0

Supplies

- Ivory wild silk: 13¾ x 12 inches (top); 12 x 10 inches (bottom)
- 13¾ x 12 inches white cotton batiste
- 12 x 10 inches batting
- 2—15¾ inches ivory silk ribbon, ⅜ inch wide
- 1 spool ivory silk sewing thread
- 1 spool ivory silk embroidery floss
- ⅓ ounce cotton stuffing
- Polyester fiberfill
- 10 x 8 inches thin rigid plastic
- Double-sided tape

Dimensions: 9½ x 6¾ inches
Patterns on the detachable pattern insert at the back of the book

Transferring

Transfer the boutis pattern to the center of the wild silk piece intended for the top, tracing the pattern through the fabric as explained on page 118. Add the initials using the alphabet on the opposite page. On a material as delicate as silk, it is preferable to use a fabric pencil or even a disappearing-ink marker.

Stitching

Place the batiste under the prepared silk, wrong sides together. Baste them together (see page 118), then place them in an embroidery hoop (see page 120).

With embroidery floss, embroider the large flowers, the knot, and the initials with backstitch, and the dots with satin stitch. Embroider all the other motifs in running stitch with sewing thread (see page 124). To embroider the medallions on the edging evenly, see the tip on page 59.

Stuffing

Turn the work over to the wrong side. Stuff the edging, motifs, and initials (see pages 122–123).

Washing

To preserve the luster of the silk, erase the lines using the steam from an iron instead of washing the piece.

Assembling

Pin the batting to the wrong side of the remaining silk and baste the perimeter. Transfer the pattern for the bottom to the plastic, inverting it to make a mirror image on both sides of the dotted line, then cut the piece out. Attach the heart in plastic to the center of the fleece with the double-sided tape. Attach the plastic heart to the center of the fleece with the double-sided tape. Cut, leaving a seam allowance of ¾ inch all the way around. Sew a gathering thread with a running stitch around the edge of the excess fabric, and pull it so that it pulls the fabric over the plastic (diagram below), then stop.

Cut out the boutis piece, keeping an allowance of ¾ inch around the edging. Working as before, gather the excess fabric so that the boutis is exactly the same size as the fleece-lined bottom.

Put the boutis on top of the bottom, batiste against plastic. Join them with ladder stitch (see page 126), leaving a 2-inch opening on one side. Fill the piece with fiberfill, then close the opening with small stitches.

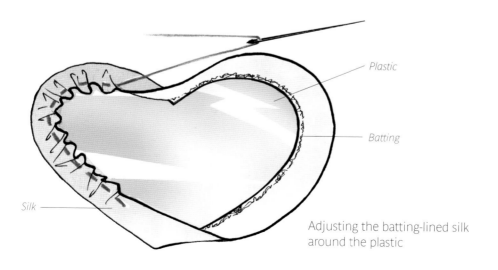

Adjusting the batting-lined silk around the plastic

Plastic

Batting

Silk

Finishing touches

Fold the ribbons in half and sew them on top of the pillow, under the initials, then tie each into a bow.

ABCDEFG
HIJKLM
NOPQRST
UVWXYZ
1234567890

Supplies

- White silk: 14¼ x 10 inches;
  4—6¼ x 8¼ inches; 2 x 8 inches
- 14¼ x 10 inches white cotton batiste
- Medium-thick batting:
  2—5¾ x 7¾ inches; ⅜ x 7¾ inches
- 1 spool ivory silk embroidery floss
- ⅓ ounce cotton stuffing
- Cardboard, about ¹⁄₁₀ inch thick
  (see cutting instructions opposite)
- Cardboard, about half as thick
  (see cutting instructions opposite)
- 2—5 x 7 inches transparent
  plastic film
- Double-sided tape
- Vinyl fabric adhesive
- All-purpose adhesive

Dimensions of the closed frame:
  5¾ x 7¾ inches
Patterns on page 41

Cutting instructions
Cardboard, about ¹⁄₁₀ inch thick
- 2—5¾ x 7¾ inches (A pieces)
- 1—⅜ x 7¾ inches (piece B)
- 2—5½ x 7½ inches (C pieces); cut a
  4 x 6-inch window out of the center.

*Cardboard, about half as thick as the
  first pieces*
- 2—5½ x 7½ inches (D pieces)

Transferring

On the 14¼ x 10-inch piece of silk, baste a vertical line indicating the middle of the long sides. Transfer the small flower motif to the center of the left half and the wreath motif to the center of the right half. Trace the pattern through the fabric or, if the fabric is too opaque, with transfer paper (see page 118). Add the initials using the alphabet on page 40 and the date using the numbers from page 31.

Stitching

Place the batiste under the prepared silk, wrong sides together. Baste them together (see page 118), then place them in an embroidery hoop (see page 120).

With the embroidery floss, embroider the motifs and initials in backstitch, the dots in satin stitch, then the date in stem stitch (see page 124).

Stuffing

Turn the work over to the wrong side. Stuff the motifs and initials (see pages 122–123).

Tip

Since silk is very delicate, it is better to transfer the motif using a fabric pencil or disappearing-ink marker. To preserve the luster of the fabric, erase the lines using the steam from an iron instead of washing the piece.

1. Placement of the cardboard pieces on the wrong side of the boutis

Washing

Wash the piece, let it dry, then iron the areas without embroidery.

Preparing the spine

Baste a ½ x 7¾-inch rectangle in the center of the piece. With running stitch, embroider the frame, then, on the inside, two other vertical lines spaced ⅜ inch apart.

Putting the cover on

With the double-sided tape, stick the batting rectangles on the pieces of cardboard A and B.

Place piece B on the wrong side of the boutis, inside the embroidered frame for the spine. Position the A pieces on either side, spacing them about ⅛ inch apart, according to the thickness of the cardboard used (diagram 1).

Cut out the boutis around the whole thing, with a seam allowance of ¾ inch. Cut the four corners at an angle 2 mm from the cardboard pieces (diagram 2). Fold the loose panels over the cardboard and tape them. Carefully mark the gaps on either side of piece B.

On the 2 x 10-inch silk strip, fold the short ends under to get a length of 7½ inches. Glue the strip onto piece B, centering it heightwise and widthwise, then mark the gaps well on both sides.

Preparing the frames

Glue a cardboard piece C on the wrong side of one of the remaining silk rectangles, centering it carefully. Cut the four corners at an angle 2 mm from the cardboard. Cut out the window, keeping a margin of ⅜ inch. Fold the four loose flaps of the window and that of one of the long sides to the back and tape them. Attach a plastic film rectangle on the back, centering it over the window. Prepare the other C piece in the same way.

Glue each D cardboard piece in the center of a silk rectangle, on the wrong side. Cut the four corners at an angle 1 mm from the cardboard. Fold back all the loose flaps and stick them to the back.

Assembling

Take a C piece with the covered side on top, and place on top of it a D piece, also with the covered side on top. Fold the three loose flaps to the back of the D piece (diagram 3). Assemble the two other pieces in the same way.

Tape the completed frames to the back of the cover, carefully centering them on the A pieces and making sure to position the long open sides toward the inside.

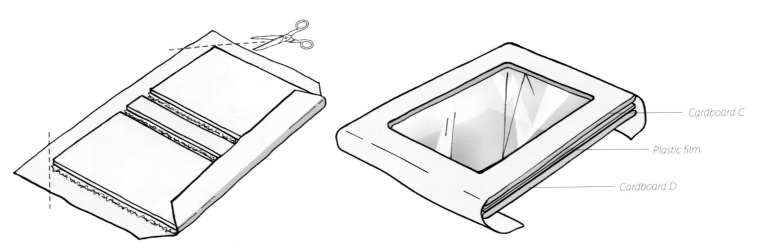

2. Assembling the cover

3. Assembling the frames

Cardboard C

Plastic film

Cardboard D

ABCDEF
GHIJKL
MNOPQ
RSTUV
WXYZ

Motif for the right half

— Backstitch

— Stem stitch

◍ Satin stitch

Motif for the left half

Boutis
for Women

Elegant Handbag

Supplies

• White cotton batiste: 4—12 x 15¾ inches (main pieces); 2—2⅜ x 19¾ inches (handles)
• 59 inches white grosgrain ribbon, 2 inches wide
• 1 spool white quilting thread
• 1¾ ounces cotton stuffing

Dimensions: 7½ x 10 x 2 inches
Pattern on pages 48–49

Transferring

Transfer the pattern to the center of two of the batiste rectangles intended for main pieces, tracing the pattern through the fabric as explained on page 118.

Stitching

Place a blank batiste rectangle under one of the prepared pieces, wrong sides together. Baste them together (see page 118), then place them in an embroidery hoop (see page 120).

Embroider all the motifs in a running stitch with quilting thread (see page 124).

Line, baste, and sew the other piece in the same way.

Stuffing

Turn the work over to the wrong side and stuff all the motifs (see pages 122–123).

Cutting

Cut the two pieces, leaving a seam allowance of ⅜ inch all the way around each, and make a rolled hem all the way around the edge.

Assembling

Fold the grosgrain ribbon in half. Sew the ends ⅜ inch from the edge. Turn the piece inside out to place the stitching inside. Pin it between the two pieces of boutis with right sides out, on the first line of stitching (diagram 1). With quilting thread doubled for more strength, sew each piece to the ribbon with ladder stitch (see page 126).

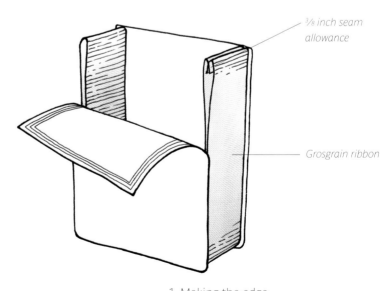

⅜ inch seam allowance

Grosgrain ribbon

1. Making the edge

Handles

Fold each of the batiste strips for the handles in half, folding the long sides together, right sides together. Stitch along the two long sides, ¼ inch from the edges. Trim the seam allowances to ²⁄₁₀ inch, then turn the pieces right side out. Embroider two rows of top-stitch on these pieces, ¼ inch from the long sides, to create three stripes (diagram 2). Stuff the three stripes along their entire length.

Roll up the ends of the handles twice and hold the coils in place with hidden stitches. Sew the handles at the top of the purse (diagram 3).

Finishing touches

Wash the purse. While it is still wet, fill it with scraps of cloth or terry cloth to give it a well-defined shape and let it dry in that shape.

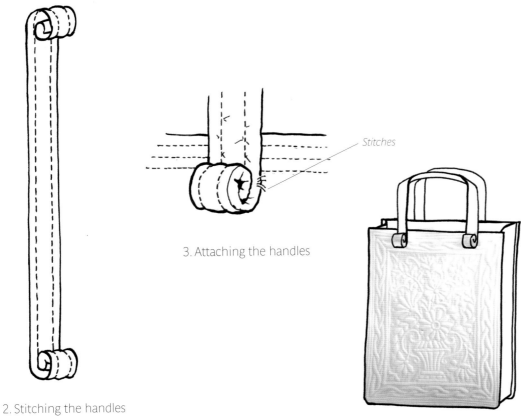

Stitches

3. Attaching the handles

2. Stitching the handles

Pattern for the top part
Put the whole pattern together by
matching up the dotted lines.

Pattern for the bottom part

Put the whole pattern together by
matching up the dotted lines.

—— Running stitch

Full pattern, smaller version

Supplies

- White cotton batiste: 2—35½ x 39⅓ (main pieces); 2—31½ x 19¾ inches (lining)
- 67 inches white satin grosgrain ribbon, ⅜ inch wide
- 1 spool white sewing thread
- 3 skeins white embroidery floss
- 1 ounce cotton stuffing

Size: 6 to 12
Patterns on the detachable pattern insert at the back of the book

Preparation

Fold the batiste rectangles for the main pieces in half, right sides together. Transfer the patterns below, leaving a margin of 2 inches at top to make it easier to stretch the piece in the hoop.

Transferring

Transfer the motifs for the back and front to the corresponding main pieces, following the outline of the neck (trace the patterns through the fabric, as explained on page 118).

Stitching

Place a blank batiste rectangle under the piece for the front, wrong sides together, aligning it at the top and centering it widthwise. Baste them together (see page 118), then place them in an embroidery hoop (see page 120).

With embroidery floss, embroider the motifs and the three lines around the armholes in backstitch, then the dots in satin stitch (see page 124).

Line, baste, and sew the back in the same way. Cut the slit in the front, then embroider its edges in buttonhole stitch with embroidery floss.

Stuffing

Turn the pieces over to the wrong side. Stuff the motifs as well as the two stripes around the neck and the armholes (see pages 122 – 123).

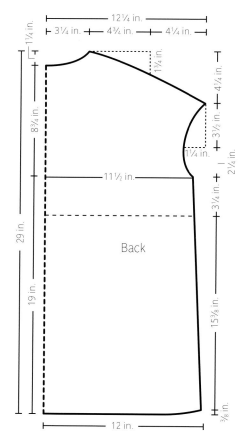

Back

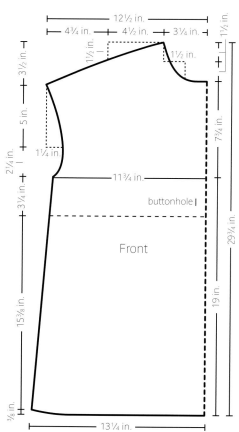

Front

Cutting

On each piece, cut the fabric of the neck, leaving a seam allowance of ³⁄₈ inch.

Cut the pieces out, keeping an allowance of 1½ inches at the bottom and ³⁄₈ inch on the rest of the edge.

Trim the lining pieces so that they reach the dotted line of the patterns.

Assembling

Sew around the edge of each piece, including the linings, with zigzag stitches.

Place the front on the back, right sides together. Pin the shoulders and the sides. Baste, then sew ³⁄₈ inch from the edges. Open the seam allowances with the iron. Make a rolled hem on the excess fabric around the neck and armholes (see page 126).

Fold the lower edge of the tunic back to the wrong side ⅓ inch, then 1 inch. Baste, then hem.

Casing

In the center of the front, on the right side, draw two buttonholes ½ inch tall, spaced 1½ inches apart (diagram 1). Sew them with embroidery floss (see page 126). All around the tunic, on the wrong side, sew a line of topstitch ¾ inch above the lower edge of the linings, then a second ¾ inch higher.

Finishing touches

Wash the tunic to erase the pencil marks. Using a safety pin, thread the grosgrain ribbon through the buttonholes and, between the two layers of fabric (diagram 2).

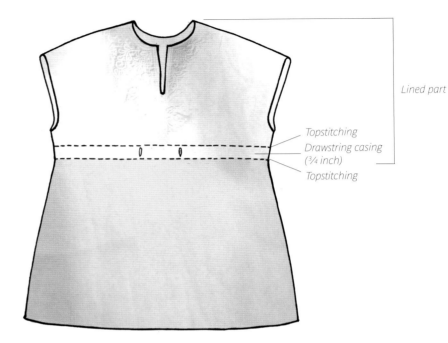

Lined part

Topstitching
Drawstring casing (¾ inch)
Topstitching

1. Making the casing

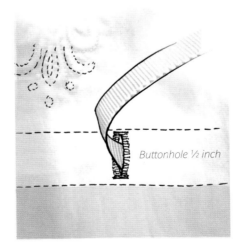

Buttonhole ½ inch

2. Threading the grosgrain ribbon

Silk Purse

Supplies

• Ivory wild silk: 12 x 17¾ inches (main piece); 10 x 15¾ inches (front)
• 12 x 17¾ inches thin fabric in white cotton (lining)
• 47¼ inches grosgrain ribbon, ½ inch wide
• 1 spool ivory silk embroidery floss
• 1 spool ivory silk sewing thread
• 1 ounce cotton stuffing

Dimensions: 6⅜ x 7¼ inches (without the strap)
Patterns on the detachable insert at the back of the book

Transferring

Tracing through the fabric, transfer the pattern for the boutis to the center of the main piece of silk (see page 118).

Stitching

Place the cotton fabric under the prepared silk, wrong sides together. Baste them together (see page 118), then place them in an embroidery hoop (see page 120).

  With embroidery floss, embroider the spirals on top and the flower motifs in backstitch; embroider the other lines in running stitch with sewing thread (see page 124). Embroider the scallops of the edging on top with buttonhole stitch with embroidery floss (see page 125).

Stuffing

Turn the work over to the wrong side. Begin the stuffing with the motifs made in backstitch, inserting two strands in them (see pages 122–123). Then stuff the bands marked out by the lines in running stitch, only stuffing them with one strand.

Washing

Erase the pencil marks using steam from an iron, which is less aggressive for silk than washing.

Cutting

Cut the fabric close to the buttonhole stitches, leaving a seam allowance of ⅜ inch on the rest of the edge.

Tip

Since silk is very delicate, it is better to transfer the pattern using a fabric pencil or disappearing-ink marker.

Preparing the front

Fold the remaining piece of silk in half, right sides together. Transfer the pattern for the front, lining up the dotted line with the fold. Cut the piece out, leaving a seam allowance of ⅜ inch all the way around. Fold in half, wrong sides together, and baste the edge. Make two darts between the * marks; baste them, then tack them into place with a few stitches on the seam line. Make a rolled hem on the seam allowance (see page 126).

Assembling

Put the boutis and front on top of one another, right sides together, lining them up at the bottom. Pin them. Fold the excess fabric of the boutis over the hem of the front and make a rolled hem, sewing through both pieces at the same time.

Finishing touches

Join the two ends of the grosgrain ribbon so that they make a ring. Sew it on the wrong side of the boutis, just above the front (diagram below).

If you want, make a tassel (see diagrams on right) and sew it to the tip of the flap.

Tip

On the boutis, it is easier to make the rolled hem if you have gathered the excess fabric of the two rounded corners beforehand.

Tassel, diagram 1

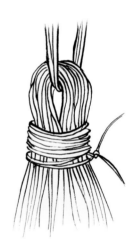

Tassel, diagram 2

Making a tassel

Cut strands of embroidery floss twice as long as the desired tassel. Hold them together in a bunch and fold it in half. Pass another strand through the loop (diagram 1). Wind embroidery floss around the bunch to form a wide tie under the loop. Fasten the thread off by tying its two ends together (diagram 2).

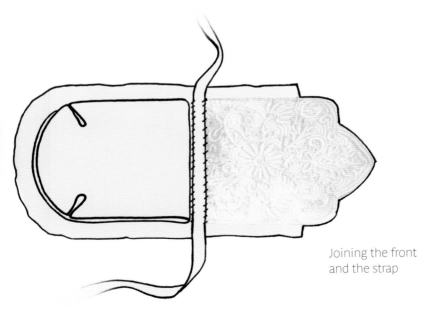

Joining the front and the strap

Eyeglass Case

Supplies

- White cotton batiste: 12 x 13¾ inches; 2—2¾ x 6¾ inches
- Bright yellow cotton fabric: 12 x 13¾ inches; 2—2¾ x 6¾ inches
- 4 x 6 inches batting
- 1 spool white quilting thread
- 1 skein white embroidery floss
- ¾ ounce cotton stuffing
- 1 snap fastener, 1 mm diameter
- 2 x 6 inches flexible plastic
- Double-sided tape

Dimensions: 6½ x 2 inches
Pattern for the main piece, page 61; pattern for the edges on the detachable pattern insert at the back of the book

Transferring

Transfer the pattern to the center of the batiste piece measuring 12 x 13¾ inches (trace the pattern through the fabric as explained on page 118).

Stitching

Place the large piece of yellow fabric under the prepared batiste, wrong sides together. Baste them together (see page 118), then place them in an embroidery hoop (see page 120).

With embroidery floss, embroider the flowers, leaves, hearts, and two circles in backstitch; embroider all the other motifs, lines, and medallions of the border in running stitch with quilting thread (see page 124). With embroidery floss, embroider the hearts of the daisy and dots in satin stitch, then the scallops of the border in button stitch (see pages 124–125).

Stuffing

Turn the work over to the wrong side. Stuff the motifs, the stripes marked out by the lines, and the medallions (see pages 122–123).

Cutting and hemming

Cut the fabric close to the buttonhole stitches, leaving a seam allowance of ⅜ inch on the rest of the edges. Make a rolled hem all along the seam allowance (see page 126).

Tip

To embroider the medallions of the border evenly, follow the line winding between each end of the ovals, then make a second line in the same way, closing the ovals this time.

End pieces

Transfer the pattern for the end pieces to the plastic two times and to the batting four times. Cut out the pieces. Use double-sided tape to attach each piece of plastic between two pieces of batting.

Put a batiste rectangle and a yellow fabric rectangle on top of one another. Center one of the end pieces on the lower half of the yellow fabric, placing the straight side at the top. Fold the two layers of fabric over the end piece (diagram 1). Pin all the layers close to the plastic. Sew around the edge in buttonhole stitch, except along the folded side. Cut the cloth close to the buttonhole stitches. Cover the second end the same way.

Assembling

Spread out the boutis horizontally, wrong side up. Place one of the end pieces on one side, behind the first line of boutis, and wrap the boutis around it so that the edges are lined up. Join with small stitches (diagram 2). Position the other end piece the same way.

Finishing touches

Wash the case to erase the pencil marks. While it is still wet, fill it with handkerchiefs or cloth to give it a well-rounded shape. Let it dry in that shape.

Sew part of the snap fastener to the underside of the flap, under the center tip, and attach the other part opposite on the right side of the front.

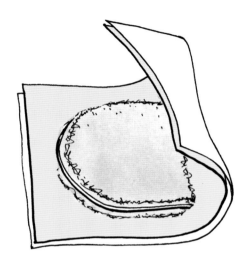

1. Covering the end pieces

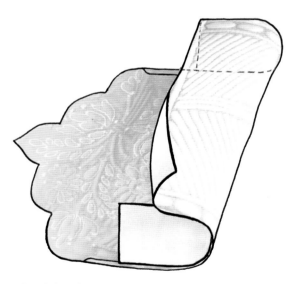

2. Joining the ends

Pattern for the main piece

— Running stitch
— Backstitch
⊘ Satin stitch
▨ Buttonhole stitch

Supplies

- White cotton batiste: 17¾ x 13¾ inches (boutis); 2—3 x 2⅜ inches (drawstring ends)
- Fuchsia cotton fabric: 17¾ x 13¾ inches (boutis); 2—6 x 4 inches (bottom); 2—3 x 2⅓ inches (drawstring ends)
- 2—6 x 4 inches batting
- 2—19¾ inches white drawstring, ⅒ inch diameter
- 1 spool white quilting thread
- 1 skein white embroidery floss
- White sewing thread
- 1 ounce cotton stuffing
- Polyester fiberfill
- 6 x 4 inches rigid plastic
- Double-sided tape

Dimensions: 5½ x 10¼ inches
Pattern for the main piece, pages 66–67; pattern for the bottom on the detachable pattern insert at the back of the book

Transferring

In the center of the batiste for the boutis, draw a 15 by 10¼-inch rectangle. Transfer the pattern for the main piece, tracing through the fabric as explained on page 118.

Preparation

With the embroidery floss, make four buttonholes on the batiste in the places indicated on the pattern (see page 126).

Fold the upper edge of the batiste along the pencil mark, wrong sides together, and iron it. In the same way, fold one of the long sides of the fuchsia fabric in the same dimensions. Place the two pieces on top of one another, wrong sides together, then join the folded sides with ladder stitch (see page 126). Trim the seam allowance to ¼ inch.

Legend for the pattern on pages 66–67

— Running stitch
— Backstitch
▬ Stem stitch
⊘ Satin stitch
▯ Buttonholes

Full pattern, smaller size

Supplies

- Solid light green cotton fabric: 35½ x 15¾ inches (main piece); 13¾ x 8 inches (bottom); 2—1¾ x 39⅓ inches (ends of the strap)
- Cotton print fabric: 35½ x 15¾ inches (lining of main piece); 13¾ x 8 inches (lining of bottom); 30¾ x 16¼ inches (inside purse); 2—1¾ x 39⅓ inches (ends of cord)
- Batting: 4—10 x 8 inches; 13¾ x 8 inches
- 2—31½-inch cord, ¼ inch diameter
- 1 spool light green quilting thread
- 1 spool quilting thread that matches the print fabric
- 1 ounce cotton stuffing
- 1 leather handle 15¾ inches long, with a 1-inch slit on each end
- 13¾ x 8 inches rigid plastic
- Double-sided tape

Dimensions: 11¾ x 5 x 11 inches (without the handle)
Patterns on the detachable insert at the back of the book

Transferring

In the center of the solid-colored fabric for the main piece, transfer the boutis pattern by inverting it on both sides of the dotted line, then repeating the half-shape on each end (diagram 1 shows the general shape that you should obtain).

Preparation

Transfer the pattern for the lower part onto each batting rectangle measuring 10 x 8 inches. Cut out the pieces and baste them on the wrong side of the prepared fabric, carefully lining them up with the marks (diagram 1).

Stitching

Place the prepared fabric and the print fabric of the same dimensions on top of one another, wrong sides together. Baste them together (see page 118), then place them in an embroidery hoop (see page 120).

With the light green quilting thread, embroider the motifs and lines in running stitch (see page 124), with the exception of the curved lines of the upper edge.

Cut the two layers of fabric along the upper edge, leaving an allowance of ⅜ inch around the line. Clip the seam allowance. With wrong sides together, fold the solid-colored fabric along the second line (in gray on the pattern), then refold the print fabric at the bottom so that it extends past the dotted line on the pattern. Embroider the three lines in running stitch.

Stuffing

Turn the work over to the wrong side. Stuff the motifs and strips marked out by the lines (see pages 122–123).

Cutting

Wash the piece to erase the pencil marks. Cut out the lower edge and the sides, leaving a seam allowance of ⅜ inch around the stitching.

Inside pouch

On the fabric for the inside pouch, make four buttonholes ½ inch high (see page 126), with the matching thread, at the places indicated in purple on diagram 2.

Fold the fabric in half, right sides together, bringing the short sides

The drawing is made on the right side of the fabric, but it is visible on this side due to the fabric's transparency.

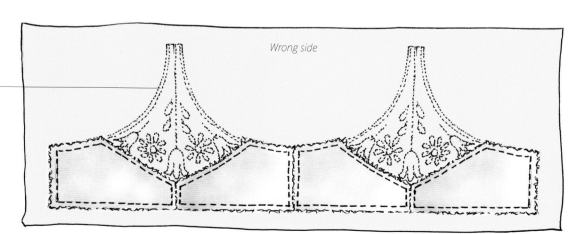

1. Placement of the batting pieces

Wrong side

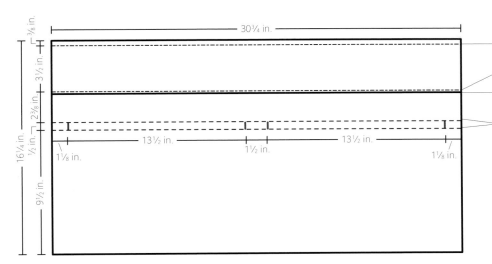

2. Diagram for the inside pouch

Fold
Fold
Running stitch line ⅛ inch under the fold
Topstitching for the casing

30¾ in.
3⅜ in.
3½ in.
2⅜ in.
½ in.
16¼ in.
9½ in.
13½ in.
1½ in.
13½ in.
1⅛ in.
1⅛ in.

3. Threading the cords

4. Attaching the handle

together. Sew them ⅜ inch from the edge, then hem the seam allowance. Fold the upper edge back to the wrong side ⅜ inch, then 3½ inches. Baste it then hem it. For the casing, sew a line of topstitch above and below the buttonholes (see diagram 2). Embroider the line indicated in the diagram in running stitch, then stuff the border obtained.

Bottom

Transfer the pattern for the bottom onto the remaining batting and plastic. Cut out the pieces and attach one on top of the other with the double-sided tape. Place them between the two pieces of fabric for the bottom, with the wrong side of the solid-colored fabric against the batting, and the wrong side of the print fabric against the plastic. Sew around the whole thing, on the edge of the plastic. Trim the excess fabric, leaving an allowance of ½ inch all the way around.

Assembling

Join the sides of the boutis piece with ladder stitch (see page 126). Make a rolled hem on the seam allowance (see page 126). Fit the bottom in the boutis piece, the solid-colored side on the outside. Join them with ladder stitch along the first line of stitching. Lay the excess fabric on the bottom.

Fold the lower edge of the pouch to the wrong side ⅜ inch. Align it with the first line of stitching on the print side of the boutis and sew it all the way around with ladder stitch. Fold the pouch against the boutis. Trim the excess fabric to ¼ inch, except for that of the print bottom. Fold over the pouch and sew it, making a rolled hem. Attach the pouch to the print side of the boutis, making some stitches on the joining seam, ¾ inch from the edge.

Finishing touches

Using a safety pin, thread the cords through the casing, one on each side of the pouch (diagram 3).

On the strips of print fabric, fold the four sides back to the wrong side ⅜ inch and iron them. Bring the two cords on one side of the pouch together, wind one strip around them, then sew the end in place with small stitches. Repeat on the other side of the pouch.

Press the edges of the strips of solid fabric to the back as before. Roll them up, slip them into the slits in the handle, then sew the ends with small stitches at the top of the boutis, on the solid-colored side (diagram 4).

Shoulder Bag

Supplies

- Solid light green cotton fabric:
  2—11¾ x 17¾ inches (main piece);
  2 x 47¼ inches (strap)
- 10 x 13¾ inches thin striped cotton
  fabric
- 1 spool light green quilting thread
- 1 skein light green embroidery floss
  (for the tassel)
- 1 ounce white cotton stuffing

Dimensions: 7 x 6¼ inches (without
the strap)
Pattern for the main piece, pages
74–75; pattern for the front on the
detachable pattern insert at the
back of the book

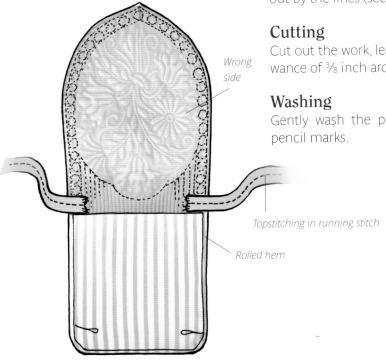

Attaching the strap

Wrong side

Topstitching in running stitch

Rolled hem

Transferring

Transfer the pattern for the main
piece to the center of one of the large
pieces of solid-colored fabric, tracing
the pattern through the fabric, as
explained on page 118.

Stitching

Put the two large pieces of solid-
colored fabric on top of one another,
wrong sides together. Baste them
together (see page 118), then place
them in an embroidery hoop (see
page 120).

Embroider the motifs and lines in
running stitch with quilting thread
(see page 124). To embroider the
medallions on the edging evenly, see
the tip on page 59.

Stuffing

Turn the work over to the wrong side.
Stuff all the motifs and strips marked
out by the lines (see pages 122–123).

Cutting

Cut out the work, leaving a seam allowance of ⅜ inch around the boutis.

Washing

Gently wash the piece to erase the
pencil marks.

Assembling

Fold the striped fabric in half, right
sides together. Transfer the pattern
for the front, lining up the dotted line
with the fold. Cut the fabric, leaving a
seam allowance of ⅜ inch all the way
around. Fold in half, wrong sides together, and baste around the edge. Make
two darts between the pattern's *
marks; baste them, then fix them in
place with a few stitches on the seam
line.

Make a rolled hem on the seam allowance on the front (see page 126). Pin
the two pieces together, wrong sides
together, lining them up at the bottom, then baste them. Fold the seam
allowance of the boutis piece over the
front and make a rolled hem around
the edge; begin with the corners, carefully rounding them, then complete
the hem at the bottom and on the
sides.

Strap

Fold the fabric for the strap in half
widthwise, wrong sides together, folding the raw edges on the long sides
to the inside. Sew along the long side
of the strip, ¼ inch from the edge.
Turn it over to the right side. With quilting thread, topstitch in running stitch
along the center of the strip to create
two equal vertical strips. Fill them with
long strands of stuffing.

Place the ends of the strap inside
inside the boutis flap, then sew them
on the wrong side of the purse (diagram on the left).

Finishing touches

Make a tassel (see page 57), then sew
it to the tip of the flap.

Pattern for the top part
Put the whole pattern together by
matching up the dotted lines.

Pattern for the bottom part
Put the whole pattern together by
matching up the dotted lines.

—— Running stitch

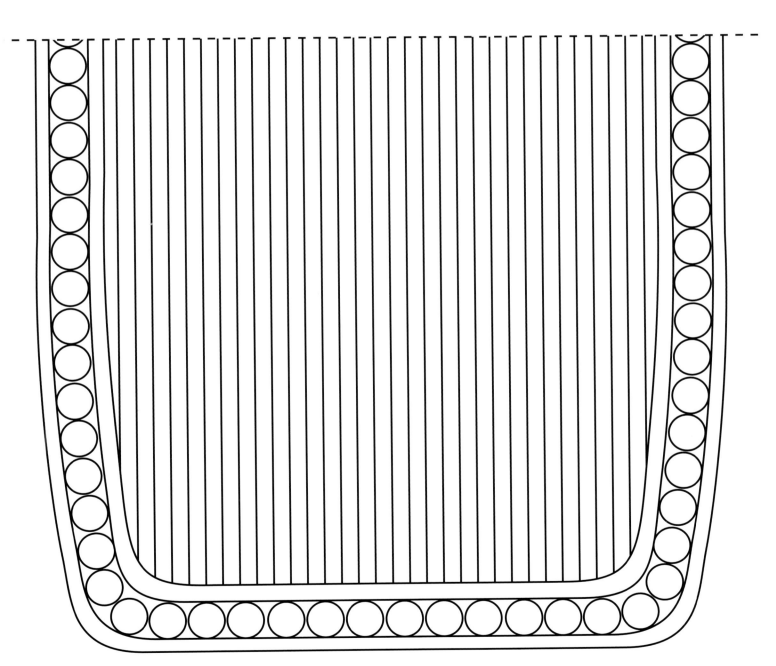

Everyday Purse

Supplies

- Beige fabric: 2—10 x 17¾ inches (main piece); 4—10 x 6 inches (inside pocket)
- 2—2⅓ inches beige ribbon, ⅜ inch wide
- 2 snap fasteners, ½ inch diameter
- 1 skein of beige quilting thread
- 1 ounce cotton stuffing
- 1 leather strap, 15¾ inches long, with snap hooks at the ends
- 8 x 2 inches flexible plastic

Dimensions: 8 x 3¾ x 1½ inches (without the strap)
Patterns on the detachable pattern insert at the back of the book

Transferring

Transfer the pattern to the center of one of the pieces of fabric, tracing the pattern through the fabric as explained on page 118.

Stitching

Place the prepared fabric on the other piece of the same size, wrong sides together. Baste them together (see page 118), then place them in an embroidery hoop (see page 120).

Embroider the motifs and lines in a running stitch with the quilting thread (see page 124).

Stuffing

Turn the work over to the wrong side. Stuff all the motifs and strips marked out by the lines (see pages 122–123).

Cutting and hemming

Wash the piece. Cut the fabric, leaving a seam allowance of ⅜ inch around the stitching. Make a rolled hem on this seam allowance, all the way around the boutis (see page 126).

Inside pocket

Transfer the pattern for the inside pocket to each of the pieces intended for this part. Cut the pieces out, leaving a seam allowance of ⅜ inch all the way around. Fold the fabric along the dotted lines, iron the fold, then unfold.

Place the two pieces on top of one another, right sides together. Pin, baste, then sew the sides and the base ⅜ inch from the edges. On each side, fold the bottom corners flat, and sew ⅜ inch from the edge (diagram 1).

Slide one of the pockets inside the other, wrong sides together. Fold the top edges inside ⅜ inch. Baste through all the layers, then sew.

Bottom

Transfer the pattern for the bottom to the plastic and cut out.

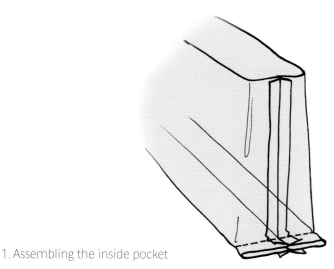

1. Assembling the inside pocket

Assembling

Spread the boutis out wrong side up. Place the plastic bottom across it, 3½ inches from the indented end. Stand the inside pocket on the bottom (diagram 2). If necessary, trim the plastic piece slightly so that it does not stick out.

Fold the main piece against the pouch and pin it. Attach the sides by sewing with small stitches between the two first lines of boutis. On the front, sew the top edges and the sides of the indentation, only stitching through the first layer of fabric, and leave the bottom free to form a pocket.

Finishing touches

Sew one part of each snap fastener on the front of the main piece, on both sides of the pocket, then attach the other parts opposite, on the wrong side of the flap.

Fold the ribbons in half. Sew them to the inside of the pocket, along the side seams.

Attach the strap's snap hooks in the ribbon loops.

Variation

You can also make the strap with beige grosgrain ribbon (see the silk purse, page 57).

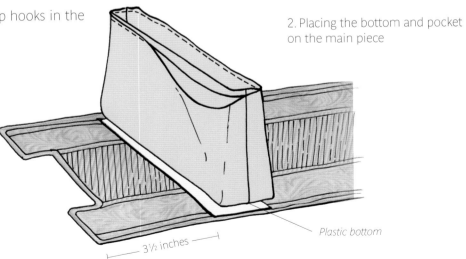

2. Placing the bottom and pocket on the main piece

Plastic bottom

3½ inches

Boutis for the Home

Supplies

- White cotton batiste: 2—
  17¾ x 17¾ inches (front); 14¼ x 11
  inches (top of back); 14¼ x 6 inches
  (bottom of back)
- 1 spool white quilting thread
- 1 skein white embroidery floss
- 1 ounce cotton stuffing, blue
- 1 square pillow, 13½ x 13½ inches

Dimensions: 14¼ x 14¼ inches
Pattern on the detachable pattern
  insert at the back of the book

Transferring

Transfer the pattern to the center of one of the batiste squares, tracing the pattern through the fabric, as explained on page 118.

Stitching

Place the two batiste squares on top of one another, wrong sides together. Baste them together (see page 118), then place them in an embroidery hoop (see page 120).

Embroider the frame in running stitch with quilting thread, and the center motif in backstitch with embroidery floss (see page 124).

Stuffing

Turn the work over to the wrong side. Stuff the motifs as well as the strips marked out by the lines of embroidery (see pages 122–123). The blue color of the stuffing creates interesting variations under the white batiste.

Cutting and hemming

Cut the piece, leaving a seam allowance of ⅜ inch around the stitching. Make a rolled hem on this allowance, all the way around the boutis (see page 126).

Assembling

On each of the pieces of batiste intended for the back, fold one of the long edges to the wrong side ¼ inch, then ⅜ inch. Sew these hems (diagram 1).

Fold the three other sides to the wrong side ⅜ inch and iron them.

Pin the shortest piece to the bottom of the boutis, wrong sides together, with the hem toward the top, lining it up with the third stuffed line. Sew the lower edge and the sides with small stitches.

In the same way, place the second piece at the top of the boutis, this time placing the hem toward the bottom, on top of the first piece (diagram 2). Sew around the sides and top edge.

Finishing touches

Wash the piece to erase the pencil marks. Slide the pillow into the cover.

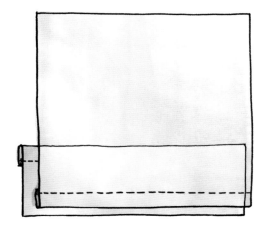

1. Hems of the back pieces

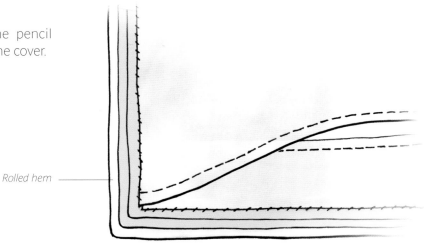

Rolled hem

2. Sewing the back pieces to the front

Supplies

- Lavender silk: 7 x 7 Inches (top); 4 x 4 inches (bottom)
- 7 x 7 inches white cotton batiste
- $2\frac{3}{8}$ x $2\frac{3}{8}$ inches batting
- $6\frac{3}{4}$ inches lavender satin ribbon, $\frac{1}{3}$ inch wide
- 1 skein purple embroidery floss
- 1 spool lavender sewing thread
- $\frac{1}{5}$ ounce cotton stuffing
- Polyester fiberfill or wool stuffing
- 4 x 4 inches rigid plastic
- Double-sided tape

Diameter: $2\frac{3}{8}$ inches
Pattern for the top on opposite page; pattern for the bottom on the detachable pattern insert at the back of the book

Tip

If possible, stuff the piece with wool or synthetic stuffing. Cotton-based materials make the needles rust more quickly.

Transferring

Transfer the pattern for the top to the center of the large silk square; trace the pattern through the fabric or, if the fabric is too opaque, use transfer paper (see page 118). On a fabric as delicate as silk, it is best to use a fabric pencil or a disappearing-ink marker.

Stitching

Place the batiste under the prepared silk, wrong sides together. Baste them together (see page 118), then place them in an embroidery hoop (see page 120).

With embroidery floss, embroider the flower in backstitch (see page 124), and the dots in satin stitch.

Stuffing

Turn the work over to the wrong side. Stuff the petals and the heart (see pages 122–123).

Cutting and washing

Cut the fabric, leaving a seam allowance of $\frac{3}{8}$ inch around the purple line of the pattern.

To preserve the luster of the silk, do not wash the piece, but erase the pencil marks with steam from an iron.

Bottom

Transfer the pattern for the bottom to the batting and plastic. Cut out the pieces and stick one on top of the other with the double-sided tape.

Transfer the pattern for the bottom to the center of the remaining silk square, on the wrong side. Sew around the edge with large stitches, $\frac{3}{8}$ inch from the line. Place the plastic and batting in the center of the silk, with the batting on the bottom. Pull the thread so that it gathers the excess over the plastic, then tie it off (diagram 1).

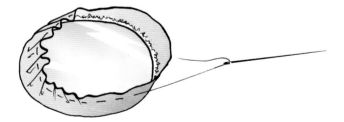

1. Gathering the bottom

Assembling

Working in the same way, gather the excess embroidered silk, ⅛ inch from the line, to give it the same diameter as the bottom (diagram 2).

Place the embroidered top and the bottom together, wrong sides together. Sew them together with ladder stitch, leaving an opening (diagram 3). Fill the piece with fiberfill or wool stuffing, then close the opening.

Finishing touches

Stitch through the center of the daisy with embroidery floss, going through all the layers, and tie the thread off securely on the bottom of the pin-cushion.

Tie the ribbon in a bow, then sew it on the seam between the top and the bottom.

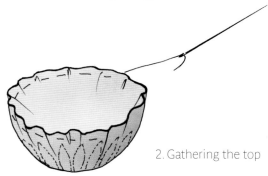

2. Gathering the top

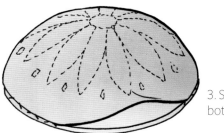

3. Sewing the top and bottom together

Pattern for the top

— Backstitch

🌀 Satin stitch

— Edge, do not embroider

Supplies

- Lavender silk: 7 x 7 inches (boutis); 6 x 6 inches (back)
- 7 x 7 inches white cotton batiste
- 2—4 x 2¾ inches batting
- 2—8¼ inches lavender satin ribbon, ⅜ inch wide
- 1 skein purple embroidery floss
- 1 spool lavender sewing thread
- ⅕ ounce white cotton stuffing
- 4 x 2¾ inches rigid plastic
- Double-sided tape

Dimensions: 2⅜ x 4⅜ inches
Pattern of the front on opposite page; pattern of the back on the detachable pattern insert at the back of the book

Transferring

Transfer the pattern for the front to the center of the large silk square, tracing the pattern through the fabric or, if the fabric is too opaque, using transfer paper (see page 118).

Stitching

Place the batiste under the prepared silk, wrong sides together. Baste them together (see page 118), then place them in an embroidery hoop (see page 120).

With embroidery floss, embroider the motifs and lines in backstitch, the dots in satin stitch, and the border in buttonhole stitch (see pages 124–125).

Stuffing

Turn the work over to the wrong side. Stuff the motifs and the band marked out by the lines (see pages 122–123).

Cutting

Cut the piece out, cutting right against the edge of the buttonhole stitches on the top edge and leaving a seam allowance of ⅜ inch around the purple line of the pattern on the rest of the edges.

Washing

Erase the pencil marks (see Tip below).

Tip

Since silk is very delicate, it is better to transfer the motif using a fabric pencil or disappearing-ink marker. To preserve the luster of the fabric, erase the lines using the steam from an iron instead of washing the piece.

Back

Transfer the pattern for the back to each piece of batting and to the plastic, then cut the pieces out. Attach the plastic between the two pieces of batting with double-sided tape.

Fold the silk for the bottom in half widthwise, right sides together. Transfer the pattern for the back to the center. Sew around the edge, leaving a long opening on one of the sides. Trim the seam allowance to ¼ inch, then clip it at regular intervals around the curves and angles. Turn the work to the right side.

Slide the batting-lined bottom into the back (diagram below). Fold the edges of the opening to the inside and close the opening with slip stitches.

Assembling

Make a rolled hem on the lower edges of the boutis piece (see page 126).

Place the boutis on the back, aligning them at the tip and on the sides. Sew them together with small slip stitches.

Finishing touches

Make a ⅜ inch hem at one of the ends of each piece of ribbon. With small stitches, sew the hemmed ends to the work. Attach one to the back of the back, behind the dip of the heart, and the other opposite on the wrong side of the boutis, only going through the first layer of fabric. Tie the ribbons in a bow to close the case.

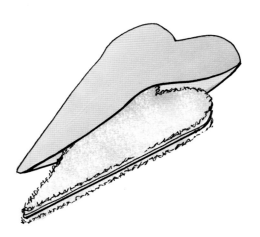

Making the back

Pattern for the front

— Backstitch

⊘ Satin stitch

▨ Buttonhole stitch

— Edge, do not embroider

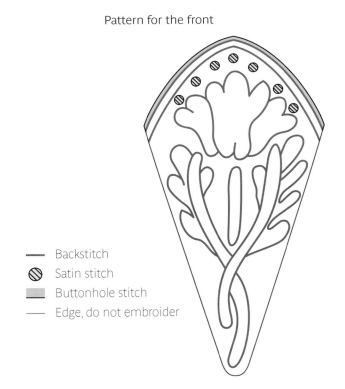

Bouquet Pillow

Supplies

- White cotton batiste: 2—
  23¾ x 23¾ inches (front);
  18½ x 14½ inches (top of back);
  18½ x 6¾ inches (bottom of back)
- 1 spool white quilting thread
- 2-3 skeins white embroidery floss
- 5¼ ounces white cotton stuffing
- 1 square pillow, 17¾ x 17¾ inches

Dimensions: 20 x 20 inches
Pattern for the border, opposite page;
  flower motifs, pages 96–97

Transferring

In the center of one of the batiste squares for the front, draw a 20 by 20-inch square. Transfer the pattern for the border to the four corners, then, using the diagram below, the diamond motifs (trace the pattern through the fabric, as explained on page 118). Draw the diagonal line connecting the top right corner with the left bottom corner, then draw parallel lines on both sides spaced 4 mm apart.

Stitching

Place the two batiste squares on top of one another, wrong sides together. Baste them together (see page 118), then place them in an embroidery hoop (see page 120).

Embroider the motifs and lines in running stitch with quilting thread, then the edging in buttonhole stitch with embroidery floss (see pages 124–125).

Stuffing

Turn the work over to the wrong side. Stuff the motifs, as well as the bands marked out by the lines (see pages 122–123).

Cutting

Cut the piece out close to the buttonhole stitches.

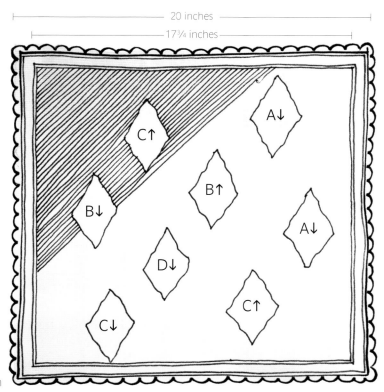

20 inches

17¾ inches

↑ Stems on top
↓ Stems on bottom

Assembling

Proceed as for the Pillow with Blue Highlights (see page 85), sewing the back pieces to the inside frame of the boutis.

Finishing touches

Wash the piece to erase the pencil marks. Slide the pillow into the cover.

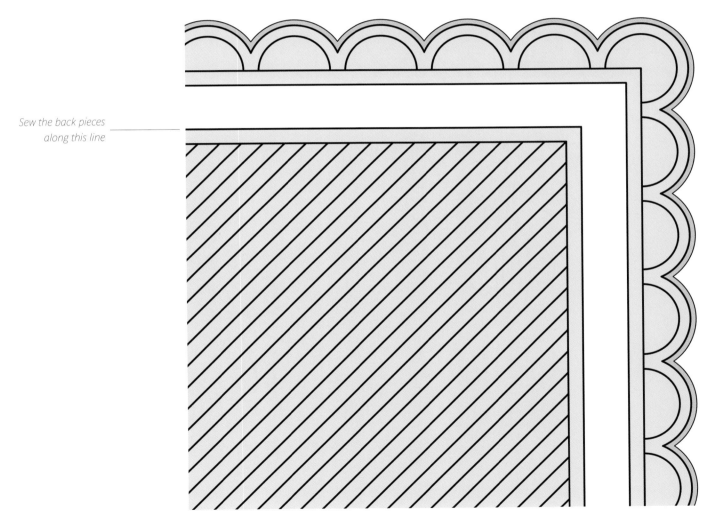

Sew the back pieces along this line

Pattern for the corners of the edging
Repeat in the four corners of the square, then fill the spaces by extending the frames and repeating the scallops (twenty on each side).

— Running stitch
▨ Buttonhole stitch
▢ Stuffing

Motif A

Motif B

— Running stitch

Motif C

Motif D

— Running stitch

Supplies

- 2—19¾ x 15¾ inches solid beige cotton fabric
- 10¾ x 7½ inches pink cotton print fabric
- 10 x 6¾ inches medium-thick batting
- 1 spool beige quilting thread
- 1 skein beige embroidery floss
- ¾ ounce cotton stuffing

Dimensions: 15¾ x 13 inches
Pattern on the detachable pattern insert at the back of the book

Preparation

Fold the four sides of print fabric to the wrong side ⅜ inch and iron the folds.

Transferring

Transfer the pattern to the center of one of the pieces of solid fabric, making a mirror image on both sides of the dotted line (do not draw the vertical lines from the center panel); trace the pattern through the fabric or, if the fabric is too opaque, use transfer paper (see page 118).

Pin the print fabric to the center panel. Baste the pieces together, then, working from the back, sew around the edge by hand or with a sewing machine. Iron, then transfer the vertical lines to the print fabric.

Stitching

On the wrong side of the solid fabric, position the batting directly above the print fabric. Sew it in place with small stitches, making sure to stitch only in the solid fabric. Place the remaining piece of solid-colored fabric on the batting with the wrong side against the batting. Baste them together (see page 118), then place the work in an embroidery hoop (see page 120).

Embroider the motifs and lines in running stitch with doubled quilting thread (see page 124), then the scallops of the corners in buttonhole stitch with embroidery floss (see page 125).

Stuffing

Turn the work over to the wrong side. Stuff the motifs and strips marked out by the lines (see pages 122–123).

Finishing touches

Cut out the piece, cutting close to the buttonhole stitches at the corners, and leaving a seam allowance of ⅜ inch on the rest of the edge. Make a rolled hem on this seam allowance (see page 126).

Wash the placemat to erase the pencil marks.

Supplies

- Pink cotton print fabric: 2—19¾ x 15¾ inches (main pieces); 8 x 6 inches (bottom)
- Solid beige cotton fabric: 2—19¾ x 15¾ inches (main pieces); 8 x 6 inches (bottom)
- Medium-thick batting: 2—13¾ x 8 (main pieces); 2—8 x 6 inches (bottom)
- 31½ inches pink satin ribbon, ⅜ inch wide
- 1 spool beige quilting thread
- 2 skeins beige embroidery floss
- 1 ounce white cotton stuffing
- 8 x 6 inches rigid plastic
- Double-sided tape

Dimensions of bottom: 6 x 4½ inches
Dimensions of the cover: 11½ x 6¼ inches (without the cuff)
Pattern for the main piece, page 103; pattern for the bottom on the detachable pattern insert at the back of the book

Transferring

Transfer the pattern for the main piece to the center of each print fabric, making a mirror image on both sides of the dotted line; trace the pattern through the fabric or, if the fabric is too opaque, use transfer paper (see page 118).

Stitching

On the wrong side of each print fabric, pin a 13¾ x 8-inch piece of batting, centering it widthwise and aligning it where indicated on the pattern. Place the solid fabric under the whole thing, the wrong side against the batting. Baste through all the layers (see page 118), then place one of the pieces in an embroidery hoop (see page 120).

Embroider the motifs and lines in running stitch (see page 124) with doubled quilting thread: work on the right side (print fabric) for the batting-lined part, and on the wrong side (solid fabric) for the top part. Working on the wrong side, embroider the scallops in buttonhole stitch with embroidery floss (see page 125).

Line, baste, and sew the other piece in the same manner.

Stuffing

Stuff the motifs and strips marked out by the lines (see pages 122–123): work from the solid side for the batting-lined part, and from the print side for the top part.

Cutting and hemming

Cut out the two pieces close to the buttonhole stitches, leaving a seam allowance of ⅜ inch on the two sides and ½ inch at the bottom.

Make a rolled hem on the seam allowance of each of the two sides (see page 126).

Bottom

Transfer the pattern for the bottom to the two remaining pieces of fabric; cut it out, leaving a seam allowance of ½ inch all the way around. Transfer the same pattern once to the plastic and twice to the batting, then cut it out along the lines.

With the double-sided tape, attach the plastic between the two pieces of batting. Put the whole thing between the two pieces of fabric, with the wrong side of both against the batting (diagram 1). Sew all the way around the edge of the piece.

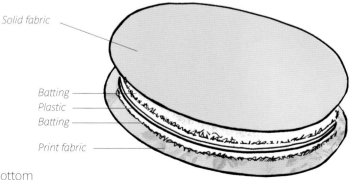

Solid fabric
Batting
Plastic
Batting
Print fabric

1. Making the bottom

Assembling

Pin the main pieces around the bottom, overlapping them in the front and back (diagram 2). Sew them on with ladder stitch (see page 126). Fold together all the layers of excess fabric around the bottom edge and make a rolled hem with them.

Washing

Wash the piece to erase the pencil marks. While it is still wet, fill it with terry cloth or handkerchiefs to shape it. Let it dry in this shape.

Finishing touches

On the solid side of each main piece, make six regularly spaced vertical buttonholes at the bottom of the top flap with embroidery floss (see page 126). Thread the ribbon through the buttonholes: it will allow you to close the cozy when the teapot is placed inside it.

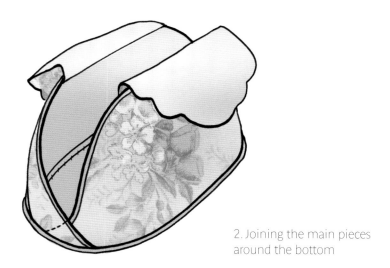

2. Joining the main pieces around the bottom

½ pattern of the tea cozy
Make a mirror image on both sides of the dotted line.

Line up the batting with this mark.

— Running stitch
▬ Buttonhole stitch

Travel Sewing Kit

Supplies

- Solid sky blue cotton fabric: 2—3¾ x 8 inches (exterior); 2 x 6⅜ inches (edge); 3¼ x 3½ inches (pincushion)
- Cotton print fabric: 2—4½ x 6½ inches (interior cardboard pieces); 8 x 8 inches (left pocket); 4¾ x 5¼ inches (right pocket);
- Medium-thick batting: 2—4 x 6 inches; ⅜ x 6 inches
- 3½ feet white satin ribbon, 2⅓ inches wide
- 1 skein sky blue embroidery floss
- White sewing thread
- ⅕ ounce white cotton stuffing
- Cardboard, about ⅒ inch thick (see cutting instructions below)
- Cardboard, about half as thick as the first piece (see cutting instructions below)
- Polyester fiberfill
- Double-sided tape
- Gummed paper tape
- Vinyl fabric adhesive

Dimensions of the kit (closed): 4 x 6 inches
Pattern on opposite page

Cutting instructions

Cardboard, about ⅒ inch thick
- 2—4 x 6 inches (A pieces)
- 1—⅜ x 6 inches (B piece)

Cardboard, about half as thick as the first piece
- 2—3¾ x 5¾ inches (C pieces)

Transferring

On one of the 13¾ x 8-inch pieces of fabric, baste a vertical line indicating the middle of the long sides. Transfer the pattern to the center of the right half; trace the pattern through the fabric or, if the fabric is too opaque, use transfer paper (see page 118).

Stitching

Place the prepared fabric on top of the solid piece of the same dimensions, wrong sides together. Baste them together (see page 118), then place them in an embroidery hoop (see page 120).

Embroider the motif with embroidery floss, in stem stitch for the circles and stems, in satin stitch for the dots, and in backstitch for the other lines (see page 124).

Stuffing

Turn the work over to the wrong side and stuff all the motifs (see page 122).

Washing

Wash the piece, let it dry, then iron the unembroidered areas.

Putting the cover on

Follow the directions for Wedding Memories, page 39 (cover the B piece with the strip of solid-colored fabric intended for the edge, cut so that it measures 5¾ inches).

Interior

Glue each piece of cardboard C to the wrong side of a piece of print fabric measuring 4½ x 6½ inches, centering it on the fabric. Cut the four corners at an angle ⅛ inch from the cardboard. Fold the loose flaps to the back and glue them there.

Left pocket

Fold the piece of 8 x 8-inch print fabric in half, wrong sides together. Make a tuck at the center. Tie an 8-inch long ribbon in a bow and sew it at the top of the tuck to hold it in place. Place the fabric on one of the cardboard pieces C, around 1¼ inches from the long side on the right, centering it height wise. Trim the excess fabric ⅜ inch from the cardboard, then glue it to the back of the latter (diagram 1).

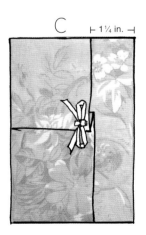

1. Left pocket

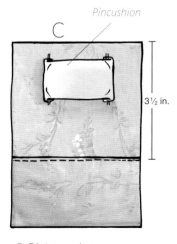

2. Right pocket

Right pocket

Fold the piece of 4¾ x 5¼-inch print fabric in half lengthwise, wrong sides together. Topstitch the fold. Place the piece on the other cardboard C, 3½ inches from the top, centering it widthwise.

Pincushion

Fold the piece of solid-colored fabric for the pincushion in half lengthwise, right sides together. Stitch the short sides ¼ inch from the edges. Turn the piece to the right side. At the two ends, fold the edges to the inside ¼ inch. Fill with fiberfill. Sew the ends close to the edges, fold them under the pincushion ¼ inch, then sew them to the back with small stitches to form casings. Sew the cushion on cardboard C on the right, passing the thread through the casings (diagram 2).

Assembling

Fold an 8-inch piece of ribbon in half. With the gummed kraft tape, attach it on the wrong side of the cover, in the center of the long side of the back. Attach two 13¾-inch ribbons to the center of the long side of the front (diagram 3).

Glue the C cardboards on the A cardboards, carefully centering them. Open the piece so that it is flat, press it, and let it dry for about twelve hours.

3. Attaching ribbons for closing

— Backstitch

— Stem stitch

⊘ Satin stitch

Motif for the front

Supplies

- Lavender silk: 2—10 x 10 inches (embroidered lids); 4—8 x 8 inches (unembroidered lids and bottom); 2—48 x 3½ inches (sides); 8 x 4 inches (inside pocket)
- 2—5x 10 inches white cotton batiste
- Medium-thick batting: 6—7 x 3½ inches; 2—7 x 7 inches
- 6½ feet lavender satin ribbon, ⅜ inch wide
- 1 skein purple embroidery floss
- Purple sewing thread
- ⅜ ounce white cotton stuffing
- Cardboard, about ¹⁄₁₀ inch thick (see cutting instructions opposite)
- Double-sided tape

Dimensions: 7 x 7 x 3 inches
Patterns on page 113

Cutting instructions
Cardboard, about ¹⁄₁₀ inch thick
- 4—7 x 3½ inches (A pieces)
- 1—7 x 7 inches (B piece)

Transferring

On each of the silk pieces intended for the embroidered lids, baste a vertical line indicating the center. On one of the pieces, transfer the right lid motif to the center of the right half; on the other, transfer the left lid motif to the center of the left half. Trace the pattern through the fabric or, if the fabric is too opaque, use transfer paper (see page 118).

Stitching

Place a batiste rectangle under one of the prepared pieces of silk, wrong sides together, centering it carefully under the motif. Baste the work together (see page 118), then place it in an embroidery hoop (see page 120).

With the embroidery floss, embroider the motifs in backstitch and the dots in satin stitch (see page 124).

Line, baste, and sew the other piece in the same way.

Stuffing

Turn the work over to the wrong side and stuff all the motifs (see pages 122–123).

Washing

Erase the pencil marks (see Tip, opposite page).

Tip

Since silk is very delicate, it is better to transfer the motif using a fabric pencil or disappearing-ink marker. To preserve the luster of the fabric, erase the lines using the steam from an iron instead of washing the piece.

Embroidered lids

With the double-sided tape, attach a piece of batting on each side of one of the A cardboard pieces. Place the cardboard on the wrong side of a boutis piece, carefully centering the motif. Cut the fabric to make a 8- by 8-inch square, with ⅜ inch of loose fabric around the cardboard. Cut the corners at a diagonal, including at both corners of the cardboard (diagram 1). Fold the loose panels of the embroidered part over the batting. Fold the panels of the unembroidered part over the wrong side, then fold that part over the batting. Close the three sides with small slip stitches.

Prepare the other lid in the same way.

Preparing the inside pocket

On the piece of silk intended for the pocket, fold the long sides ⅜ inch to the wrong side, then fold the piece in half widthwise to get a piece 8 x 1½ inches.

Unembroidered lids

With the double-sided tape, attach a piece of batting over one of the sides of the two remaining A cardboard pieces.

Place a cardboard piece on the wrong side of a 8 x 8-inch silk square, with the batting-lined side on top, leaving ⅜ inch of fabric loose over three sides. Cut the corners at a diagonal and fold the silk over to the back, as with the embroidered lids. Align the long open side of the pocket with that of the lid. Fold its ends ⅜ inch and slip them between the folded part and the batting. Embroider some decorative stitches in the center of the long folded side of the pocket, sewing through the silk below at the same time, to create two compartments. Close the three sides of the lid, sewing through all the layers.

Cover the last piece of cardboard in the same way, but without a pocket. Before closing the short sides, slip an 8-inch-long ribbon between the folded part and the batting at the center of the side.

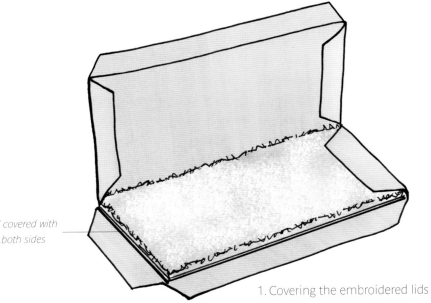

Cardboard covered with batting on both sides

1. Covering the embroidered lids

Bottom

With the double-sided tape, attach a piece of batting to each side of the B cardboard. Center the whole thing on the wrong side of one of the remaining silk squares. Cut the corners at a diagonal, then fold the loose panels over the batting. On the last silk square, fold the four sides to the wrong side ⅜ inch. Place this square on the batting, then join it to the other with slip stitch all around the outside of the cardboard.

Sides

Fold one of the silk rectangles for the sides in half widthwise, right sides together. Stitch the side opposite the folded edge ⅜ inch from the edge. Turn the piece over to the right side. Fold the upper and lower edges to the wrong side ⅜ inch. Prepare the other piece the same way. Slip it in the first, right sides together, lining up the seams and tucks. Beginning on the seams, stick a pin in the top edge every 12 inches. Using basting thread, gather all the layers from one pin to the next until you have four sections, each 7 inches long. Gather the lower edge in the same way.

Assembling

Working with slip stitches, sew the lower edge of the sides around the bottom, then sew the lids around the top edge, making sure to place the batting-lined sides of the unembroidered lids upward (diagram 2). Remove the basting threads.

Finishing touches

Cut the remaining ribbon into two equal lengths. Roll each of them up, leaving 13¾ inches free at the end. Sew the rolls with small hidden stitches on the embroidered lids, in the center of the long inner sides, ⅜ inch from the edge.

Thread the small spools of thread on the ribbons of the unembroidered lid, then tie the ribbons in a bow.

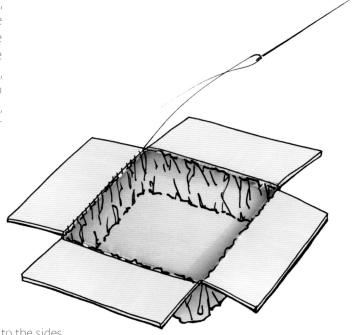

2. Joining the lids to the sides

Pattern for the left lid

Pattern for the right lid

— Backstitch

◎ Satin stitch

A Boutis Lesson
from Kumiko

Essential supplies

Threads

- 100% cotton sewing thread for running stitch. Quilting thread or waxed thread is usually used to achieve a sturdier result.
- 100% cotton embroidery floss for backstitch, blanket stitch, and buttonhole stitch. For best results, use DMC Broder Special floss, size 20 or 25.
- Cotton stuffing. It can be 100% cotton or a cotton/synthetic mix, like unplied knitting yarn. Keep in mind that pure cotton is 10–15% heavier than a cotton/synthetic mix. Never use wool, which it loses its shape when you wash it.

Fabrics

The fabric must be thin but sturdy enough to withstand the stitching and stuffing.

- Traditionally, boutis quilting is done with white batiste. Batiste is a fine, light linen weave. Originally, it only existed in linen but today it is also available in combed cotton and mercerized cotton. Use unprocessed 100% cotton batiste.
- Percale is a fine closely woven cotton fabric. It has been treated, giving it a slightly shiny appearance and a certain stiffness.
- Cotton sheet linen is a simple and inexpensive option.
- If you use other fabrics, for example, cotton quilting fabric or wild silk, try embroidering or stuffing on a scrap before beginning the project.

Tools

- Needles. Use a sewing needle or very fine quilting needle to work with the sewing thread; an embroidery needle to work with the embroidery floss; and a yarn needle—that is, one with a round end—(no. 16 or no. 18) to tuck ends under the fabric.
- Hoops. For small pieces, use an embroidery hoop of about 6 inches in diameter because, since it smaller than your hand, it provides good support. If you work on larger pieces, choose a quilting ring, which is thicker than an embroidery hoop.
- A soft (HB) lead pencil for transferring the motif and a mechanical pencil with 0.7 mm lead for thin lines or fragile fabrics.
- 2 thimbles with rims (one for the middle finger or index finger of each hand).
- Wooden toothpicks to push the cotton stuffing inside the piece.
- A ruler
- A pair of sewing scissors to cut the fabric around the motifs.
- A pair of embroidery scissors to cut threads, take out hemstitches, and trim close to blanket or buttonhole stitches.
- Soap for washing. Marseille soap (*savon de Marseille*) is traditionally used, but you can use any gentle detergent.

Tip

For very delicate pieces, do not hesitate to use less cotton stuffing.

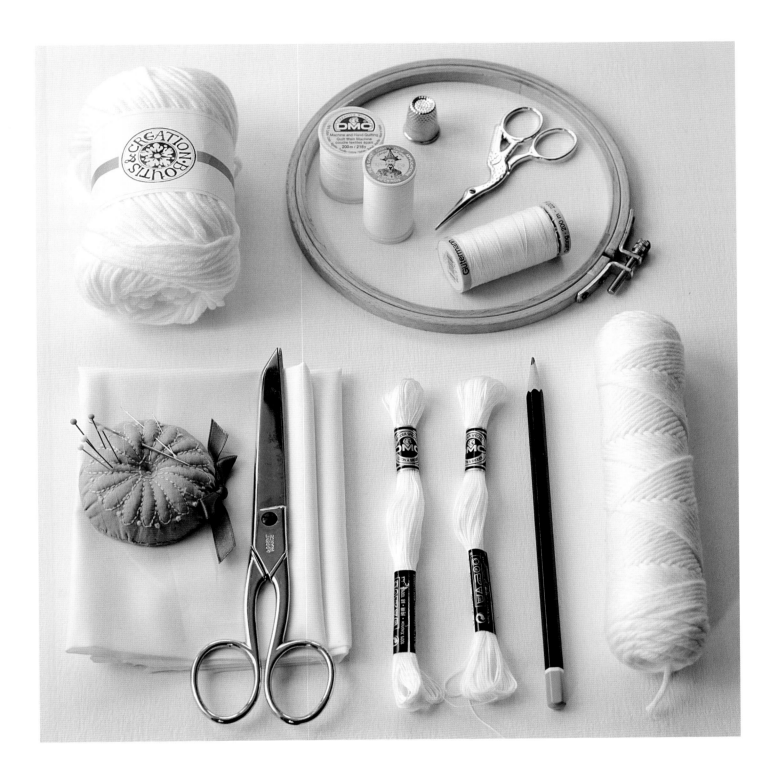

Basic boutis techniques

The art of boutis lies entirely in the effects of transparency and the quality of the stitches. Practice the basics of boutis by making this card holder. In a few steps, you can make this pretty object, which will protect your business cards or debit and credit cards, and at the same time learn the essential techniques of this craft.

Supplies

In addition to the essential tools listed on page 116, you will need:
• 2—15¾ x 10 inches white 100% cotton batiste
• 1 spool white quilting thread
• 1 skein white embroidery floss
• ⅓ ounce white cotton stuffing

Tip

You can create interesting variations by choosing a lining fabric in a bright color. The background of the piece will then take on a pastel hue and the boutis will appear in white (see Eyeglass Case on page 58 or A Taste of Japan on page 62).

Transferring the pattern

Make a photocopy of the pattern provided on page 121. Place one of the pieces of batiste (or the main fabric selected) on the photocopy, on the right side, orienting it in the direction of the grain of the fabric (that is, parallel to the selvages). Because the fabric is so thin, you should be able to see the pattern through it. Pin the photocopy and fabric together, then trace the motif with a regular pencil or a mechanical pencil. Always work from the center to the outside, especially when working on a large project, to avoid bad joints when you move the piece on the work surface.

If the fabric proves to be too thick or opaque to see through, use transfer paper for textiles (follow the manufacturer's instructions).

When you use transfer paper, go back over the motifs lightly in red as you transfer them to keep track of where you are.

Basting

By definition, a boutis piece consists of two layers of fabric, between which you slip strands of stuffing to achieve a distinctive raised effect.

Spread the main fabric (which will be on its right side) over the lining fabric, wrong sides together. Baste them together with quilting thread, making a grid pattern of lines 2 to 2⅜ inches apart (diagram below). This preparation is very important: not only does it hold the two layers of fabric in place but it creates invaluable reference lines for the rest of the work.

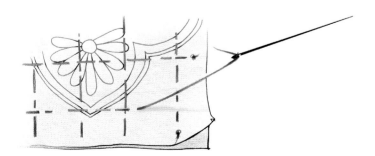

Stitching

Place the basted fabric in the embroidery hoop, right side up. First stretch it smoothly between the two rings then slowly tighten the screw while gradually stretching the fabric around its entire perimeter.

Put a thimble on the middle or index finger of each hand. Visible under the fabric, the rim of the thimble makes it easier to perform more precise stitches.

Always choose a thread that is the same color as the fabric to achieve the delicacy of traditional pieces. The stitching is done on the right side of the fabric.

Tie a knot at the end of the thread. Insert the needle in the main fabric ½ inch from the line and come out on that line (diagram 1). Pull the needle with a tug so that the knot is pulled between the two pieces of fabric (diagram 2).

Make a small backstitch, then continue, using the type of stitch recommended in the model. In any case, always make small, regular stitches. To make sure the stitches are good and tight, lift the fabric slightly with the hand that is not holding the needle.

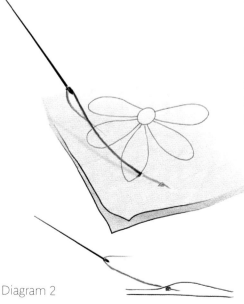

Diagram 1

Diagram 2

^ ⅔ inch

Tip

A simple method for tying a knot is to wrap the thread around the needle twice then pull the needle, holding the thread with your finger.

Once you have finished sewing one line, move on to the next, without cutting the thread. It is essential that you do not sew the two fabrics together in places that will later be stuffed. To move from one area to another, simply slip the needle in between the two layers of fabric and come back out at the desired place.

As you stitch, you can remove the basting threads.

To end a length of thread, make a small backstitch, then tie a knot. Insert the needle in the main fabric, bring it out ½ inch away, then give the needle a little tug to catch the knot between the two layers as before.

Embroidery

This small card holder is a good exercise for beginners because it requires several of the stitches most commonly used in boutis. As indicated on the legend on the opposite page, the outer edges are embroidered in running stitch (with the quilting thread); the floral motif and inside lines are made in backstitch, the diagonal quilting lines in Vauvert stitch, and the edging in buttonhole stitch (with the embroidery floss). All of these stitches are explained on pages 124–125.

Pattern for the card holder

— Running stitch

— Backstitch

- - Vauvert stitch

▨ Buttonhole stitch

Stuffing

Stuffing consists of sliding a length of cotton fiber between two layers of fabric to raise certain parts of the motif. This fiber is called a "strand."

Stuffing is always done on the wrong side of the fabric, so turn your work over in the embroidery hoop.

To ensure that the strand slides through the fabric easily without ruining it, it is not threaded directly in the needle; instead a "lasso" is used. Cut a piece of quilting thread 8-10 inches long and thread it in the tapestry needle. Fold it in two, tie the end at least twice, then check the strength of the knot. Cut a somewhat short strand (around 8 inches) and put it through the lasso (diagram 1).

Slide the needle between the two pieces of fabric at the edge of the area you want to stuff (here, a daisy petal) and bring it out on the other side of the motif (diagram 2). Very gently pull the strand so that it comes between the two layers. Cut it at the edge of the fabric, making sure to preserve the lasso.

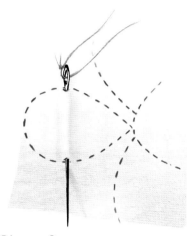

Diagram 2

Diagram 1

Note

On these two pages, the strands and embroidery stitches are shown in blue to make the diagrams easier to understand.

Repeat the step until you have created an even raised area (diagrams 3 and 4). On the motif that we are using as an example, each petal requires three or four passages, but that can vary depending on the project.

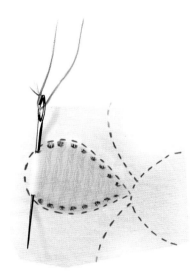

Diagram 3

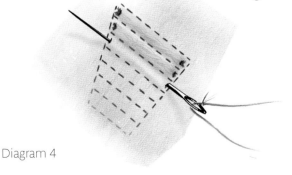

Diagram 4

If some strands protrude a little, push them back in using a wooden toothpick (diagram 5) or pull them from the inside with the tip of the needle.

Proceed in the same way for the heart of the daisy. The method can be adapted, however, depending on the motifs. Since the contour here is circular, it is impossible to stuff it in a single step. Start by passing through a portion of the edge. Pull out the needle and lasso without bringing the strand out. Insert the needle and lasso into the same hole they just came out of, then come up a little farther on. Repeat the step three or four times to go all the way around the circle, stopping just before the starting hole. The holes from the needle and lasso will disappear when washed.

Certain motifs, like the one here, are difficult to stuff regularly in one go and require a second passage. Leave a little strand at the end, then tuck it in using the wooden toothpick.

On the right side of the fabric, the stuffed parts are detached from the bottom. The effect is accentuated if you have used a main fabric and lining that are different colors.

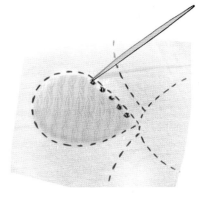

Diagram 5

Tip

You can give your boutis a nice color by selecting cotton stuffing in a bright color. The color will be softened by the main fabric but will bring out the stuffed motif (see the Pillow with Blue Highlights, page 82).

Embroidery stitches

Unless otherwise indicated, work from right to left if you are right-handed, and vice versa.

Running stitch

This is the basic stitch for sewing. Pull out the needle at 1, insert it a few millimeters away at 2 and pull it back out at 3. The stitches and spaces must always be the same length.

Stem stitch

Like backstitch, stem stitch is often used to bring out details. Work from left to right. Pull the needle out at 1, insert it a few millimeters away at 2, and pull it back out at 3, halfway between 1 and 2.

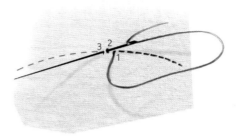
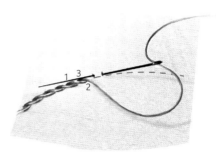

Backstitch

This stitch is used to accentuate the details because it creates a more delicate effect than running stitch. For example, on the card holder, it is used to make the floral motifs stand out. Pull the needle out at 1, insert it behind the first hole at 2, then pull it back out at 3, a few millimeters in front of the thread.

Satin stitch

Work from left to right. Stitch from one edge of the motif to the other, closely juxtaposing the stitches so that they form a dense, flat area.

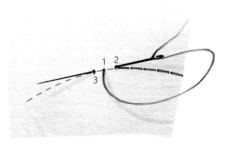
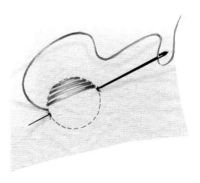

Vauvert stitch

This stitch is used to create a quilted effect. It consists of making groups of backstitches a few centimeters apart all along a line. It is important to stagger the groups from one line to the other. Afterward, you stuff diagonally between the stitches.

Blanket stitch

Because of its sturdiness, blanket stitch is used for open edges. Work from left to right. Pull the needle out at 1, insert it at 2 (the space between 1 and 2 determines the width of the edging), and pull it back out at 3, on the same line as 1, passing the thread under the needle to catch it along the edge.

Buttonhole stitch

Buttonhole stitch is identical to blanket stitch but with stitches that are closer together.

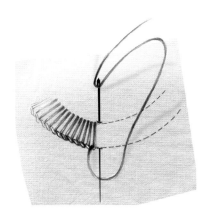

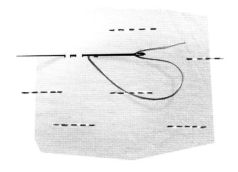

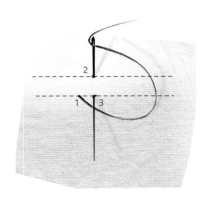

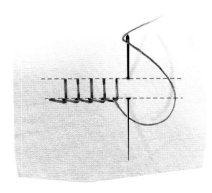

Note

Buttonhole stitch was used for all edges in this book, but you can also use blanket stitch instead.

Seam

Ladder stitch

This is a seam stitch that is made on the wrong side of a piece. Make running stitches along the edge, alternating the stitches between the two pieces to be joined. The stitches must be tight and the thread a little taut.

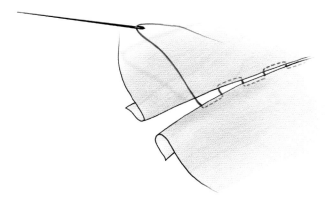

Rolled hem

Roll the excess fabric between the thumb and index finger on your left hand (or right hand if you are left-handed). Sew along the edge of this roll with blind stitches.

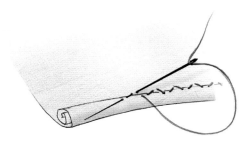

Button loop

Bring the needle out on the right side close to the edge of the piece. Insert it back into the fabric a little ways away and pull the needle through, slipping a pencil under the stitch to catch a loop. Make two other loops in the same way. Buttonhole stitch through all three loops together, repeating until the entire loop is covered by buttonhole stitch.

Making a buttonhole

Outline the shape of the buttonhole (diameter of the button x thickness of the button), then stitch on the line. Slit it in the middle with a seam ripper and continue with a pair of scissors. Embroider around the edge in buttonhole stitch, and make a bar tack at each end of the slit: Cast the thread several times over the entire width of the buttonhole, then pull it up very tight, catching a little fabric. End the thread on the wrong side.

Making bias tape

On the wrong side of the fabric, draw a strip in the dimensions indicated, at a 45° angle in relation to the grain (that is, in relation to the selvages). Cut it. Fold the long sides to the center, wrong sides together, and iron them. Unfold the strip. The folds will serve as a guide for joining the bias tape to the work.

Finishing touches

Follow the directions given in the step-by-step instructions for each project. To complete your card holder, proceed as described below.

Washing

Wash the piece with a soft brush and Marseille soap (or a gentle detergent) to erase the pencil marks. Do not wring it but dab it with a sponge, then let it air dry. Do not iron it, which may damage the fabric. Instead, gently spread it out while it is still damp. If ironing is absolutely necessary, always do it on the wrong side.

Cutting

Once the piece is dry, cut the fabric close to the buttonhole stitches. On the edges that do not have buttonhole stitch, leave a seam allowance of ⅜ inch.

Assembling

Fold the piece with right sides together, folding the lower edge up to the scallops. Pin the sides, then join them with a ladder stitch in quilting thread. Make a rolled hem on each seam allowance, as explained on the opposite page. Turn the work over to the right side.

Note

Washing and drying can shrink boutis pieces by 10 to 15%. Keep this in mind with accessories or clothes (such as A Tunic for Her, page 52) and plan to enlarge the pattern a little if necessary.

Acknowledgments

• •

The author would like to thank:
Ikuko Kimiji Ma
Kyoko Sugiura
Masako Tani
Masumi Nakamura
Rosa Cruz
Yoko Akiyama

The publisher would like to thank:
Anne, Antoine, and Simon, who welcomed the entire team in their apartment.
Blanc d'ivoire • www.blancdivoire.com
Le monde sauvage • www.lemondesauvage.com
Maison Sajou • www.sajou.fr
Stof • www.stof.fr

Published by
STACKPOLE BOOKS
5067 Ritter Road
Mechanicsburg, PA 17055
www.stackpolebooks.com

Printed in the United States

First edition

10 9 8 7 6 5 4 3

Editorial Direction: Guillaume Pô
Editing: Julie Cot and Catarina Iskyender
Artistic Direction: Chloé Eve
Illustrations: Iwona Séris
Patterns: Marie Pieroni
Technical Rewriting and Layout: Marie Pieroni
Photography: Fabrice Besse
Design: Sylvie Beauregard
Production: Sabine Marioni
Translation: Jane Wolfram
Cover design: Caroline Stover

Library of Congress Cataloging-in-Publication Data

Nakayama-Geraerts, Kumiko, 1960 –
  [Art du boutis. English]
  The art of boutis : 20 French quilting projects / Kumiko Nakayama-Geraerts ; photography, Fabrice Besse ; Design, Sylvie Beauregard. — First edition.
     pages cm
  ISBN-13: 978-0-8117-1288-0 (pbk.)
  ISBN-10: 0-8117-1288-5 (pbk.)
1. Dress accessories. 2. Trapunto—Patterns. 3. House furnishings. 4. Quilting—France. I. Title.
  TT649.8.N35 2013
  746.46—dc23
                                     2013028382